W9-BPQ-005

Also by Gia-fu Feng and Jane English:

LAO TSU/TAO TE CHING

By Gia-fu Feng (with Jerome Kirk):

TAI CHI—A WAY OF CENTERING—& I CHING

CHUANG TSU
INNER CHAPTERS

PHOTOGRAPHY BY JANE ENGLISH

CALLIGRAPHY BY GIA-FU FENG

CHUANG TSU | INNER CHAPTERS

A NEW TRANSLATION BY GIA-FU FENG AND JANE ENGLISH

VINTAGE BOOKS   A DIVISION OF RANDOM HOUSE, NEW YORK

VINTAGE BOOKS EDITION, March 1974

Copyright © 1974 by Gia-fu Feng and Jane English

All rights reserved under International and Pan-American Copyright
Conventions. Published in the United States by Random House, Inc.,
New York, and simultaneously in Canada by Random House of
Canada Limited, Toronto. Originally published by Alfred A. Knopf,
Inc., in 1974.

Library of Congress Cataloging in Publication Data:

Chuang-tsu.   Inner chapters.

Translation of a portion of Nan-hua chen ching.   I.   Title.
[BL1900.C5F38   1974b]   299'.5148'2   73–20292
ISBN 0–394–71990–5

Cover photograph by Jane English.
Cover design by Clint Anglin.
The photograph of Jane English on page 163 is by Sue Blacker.

Manufactured in the United States of America

CONTENTS

CHUANG TSU

Very little is known about Chuang Tsu and that little is inextricably woven into legend. It is said that he was a contemporary of Mencius, an official in the Lacquer Garden of Meng in Honan Province around the fourth century B.C. Chuang Tsu was to Lao Tsu as St. Paul was to Jesus and Plato to Socrates. He developed the doctrines of Taoism with rigorous logic. His fables and humor are imaginative and poetic, reflecting a brilliant and original mind. He advocated relativity with regard to all standards and values. He is at once a mystic and a revolutionary.

The rhythm of life and its organic vision, an idea poetically implied by Lao Tsu, is brought to perfect expression in the writings of Chuang Tsu. While the other philosophers were busying themselves with the practical matters of government and rules of conduct, Chuang Tsu transcended the *whang cheng*, the illusory dust of the world—thus anticipating Zen Buddhism and laying the metaphysical foundation for a state of emptiness or ego transcendence. With imagery and fantasy, he captures the depth of Chinese thinking.

The seven "Inner Chapters" presented in this translation are accepted by scholars as being definitely the work of Chuang Tsu. Another twenty-six chapters are of questionable origin; they are interpretations and developments of his teaching and may have been added by later commentators.

CHUANG TSU
INNER CHAPTERS

逍遙游

CHAPTER ONE

HAPPY WANDERING

北冥有魚其名為鯤鯤之大不知其幾千里也
化而為鳥其名為鵬鵬之背不知其幾千里也怒而
飛其翼若垂天之雲是鳥也海運則將徙於南冥
南冥者天池也齊諧者志怪者也諧之言曰鵬之
徙於南冥也水擊三千里摶扶搖而上者九萬里
去以六月息者也野馬也塵埃也生物以息相吹也
天之蒼蒼其正色邪其遠而無所至極耶
其視下也亦若是則已矣且夫水之積也不厚
則其負大舟也無力覆杯水於坳堂之上則芥為之舟
置杯焉則膠水淺而舟大也風之積也不厚則其負大翼也無力
故九萬里則風斯在下矣而後乃今培風背負青天而莫之夭閼者
而後乃今將圖南

In the Northern Ocean there is a fish called Kun which is many thousand li in size. It changes into a bird named Peng whose back is many thousand li in breadth. When it rises and flies, its wings are like clouds filling the sky.

When this bird moves across the ocean, it heads for the South Sea, the Celestial Lake. In Chi Hsieh's record of wonders it says: "When Peng is heading toward the Southern Ocean it splashes along the water for three thousand li. It rises with the wind and wings its way up to ninety thousand li; it flies for six months, and then it rests." Heat shimmers in the air like galloping horses, dust floats like the morning mist, and living creatures are blown about in the sky.

The sky is blue. Is that really so? Or does it only look blue because it stretches off into infinity? When Peng looks down from above, it will also seem blue. A large boat draws a great deal of water. Pour a cup of water into a hollow in the ground, and a mustard seed can float there like a little ship. Place the cup in it, and it will not move, because the water is shallow and the boat is large. Only at a certain height is there enough air space for a great wingspan. So Peng rises to ninety thousand li, and there is enough air below him. Then he mounts the wind, and with the blue sky at his back, and nothing in his way, he heads for the south.

蜩與學鳩笑之曰我決起而飛槍榆枋時則不至而控於地而已矣

奚以之九萬里而南為莽蒼者三飡而反腹猶果然適百里者宿舂糧

適千里者三月聚糧之二蟲又何知小知不及大知小年不及大年奚以知其然也

朝菌不知晦朔蟪蛄不知春秋此小年也楚之南有冥靈者以五百歲為春五百歲為秋

上古有大椿者以八千歲為春八千歲為秋而彭祖乃今以久特聞眾人匹之不亦悲乎

A cicada and a young dove laugh at Peng, saying, "When we try hard we can reach the trees, but sometimes we fall short and drop on the ground. How is it possible to rise ninety thousand li and head south?" If you go into the country, you take enough food for three meals and come back with your stomach as full as ever. If you travel a hundred li, you grind enough grain for an overnight stay. If you travel a thousand li, you must have three months' supply. What do these two small creatures know? Little knowledge is not to be compared with great knowledge, nor a short life with a long life.

How do we know this is so?

The morning mushroom knows nothing of twilight and dawn, nor the chrysalis of spring and autumn. These are the short-lived. South of Chu there is a ming-ling tree whose spring is five hundred years and autumn five hundred years. A long time ago there was a tortoise whose spring was eight thousand years and autumn eight thousand years. Peng Chu is a man famous for his long life. Isn't it sad that everyone wants to imitate him?

湯之問棘也是已。窮髮之北有冥海者、天池也。有魚焉、其廣數千里、未有知其修者、其名為鯤。有鳥焉、其名為鵬、背若泰山、翼若垂天之雲、摶扶搖羊角而上者九萬里、絕雲氣、負青天、然後圖南、且適南冥也。斥鴳笑之曰、彼且奚適也。我騰躍而上、不過數仞而下、翱翔蓬蒿之間、此亦飛之至也。而彼且奚適也。此小大之辯也。故夫知效一官、行比一鄉、德合一君、而徵一國者、其自視也亦若此矣。而宋榮子猶然笑之。且舉世而譽之而不加勸、舉世而非之而不加沮、定乎內外之分、辯乎榮辱之境、斯已矣。彼其於世未數數然也。雖然、猶有未樹也。夫列子御風而行、泠然善也、旬有五日而後反。彼於致福者、未數數然也。此雖免乎行、猶有所待者也。若夫乘天地之正、而御六氣之辯、以遊無窮者、彼且惡乎待哉。故曰、至人無己、神人無功、聖人無名。

In the dialogue of Tang and Chi there is the same story: "In the barren north there is a dark sea, the Celestial Lake. There is a fish living there several thousand li in breadth and no one knows its length. Its name is Kun. And there too lives a bird called Peng. Its back is like Mount Tai and its wings are like clouds across the heavens. It spirals up to ninety thousand li, beyond the clouds and the wind, and with blue sky above it heads south to the South Sea. A quail by the marsh laughs, saying, 'Where does he think he is going? I bob up and down a few feet, fluttering among the weeds and bushes. This is perfection in flying. What is he up to?' This is the difference between small and great."

Thus, those who are wise enough to hold an official position, fair enough to keep the peace in a community, virtuous enough to be a ruler and govern a state, look upon themselves in the same way.

Yet Sung Yung Tsu laughs at them. For if the whole world praised him he would not be moved. If the whole world blamed him he would not be discouraged. He knows the difference between that which is within and that which is without. He is clear about honor and disgrace. But that is all. Though such a man is rare in the world, he is still imperfect.

Lieh Tsu rode on the wind, light and at ease, and returned after fifteen days. Men as happy as he are rare. Though he no longer needed to walk, he still depended on something. But suppose someone rides on the flow of heaven and earth and the transformation of the six elements and wanders in the infinite. On what is he dependent?

Therefore it is said, "The perfect man has no self, the holy man has no merit, the sage has no reputation."

Yao thought he would cede the empire to Hsu Yu, saying, "When the sun and moon are shining, isn't it hard to see a torch? When the rainy season starts, isn't it a waste of labor to continue to water the fields? If you take over, the empire will be well ruled. I am now the ruler, and I feel inadequate. May I give the empire into your care?"

Hsu Yu said, "You are ruling the empire and the world is already at peace. If I took your place, I would be doing it for the name. Name is only the shadow of reality. Do I want to be just a shadow? The sparrow building its nest in the deep wood occupies but a single twig. The muskrat drinks only enough from the river to fill its belly. Go in peace, my lord. I have no use for the empire. If the cook at a ritual ceremony is not attending to the food offerings, the priests and the representatives of the dead do not leap over the wine and the meat to take his place."

堯讓天下於許由曰日月出矣而爝火不息其於光也不亦難乎
時雨降矣而猶浸灌其於澤也不亦勞乎夫子立而天下治
而我猶尸之吾自視缺然請致天下許由曰子治天下
天下既已治也而我猶代子吾將為名乎名者實之賓也
吾將為賓乎鷦鷯巢於深林不過一枝偃鼠飲河
不過滿腹歸休乎君予無所用天下為
庖人雖不治庖尸祝不越樽俎而代之矣

Chien Wu questioned Lien Shu: "I heard Chieh Yu telling strange stories, long and fantastic, going on and on without end. I was amazed at his words. They seemed to be as boundless as the Milky Way and had no connection with the way things really are."

Lien Shu asked, "What did he say?"

"Far away on Mount Ku lives a holy man. His flesh and skin are like ice and snow; he is as gentle as a young girl. He eats none of the five grains, but takes deep draughts of the wind and drinks the dew. He rides on clouds and mounts a flying dragon and wanders beyond the four seas. By using his spiritual powers he can protect creatures from sickness and decay, and ensure a rich harvest. I think this is ridiculous and do not believe it."

Lien Shu said, "So it is. The blind cannot appreciate beautiful patterns, the deaf cannot hear the sounds of bells and drums. Blindness and deafness are not just physical; they can be mental too. Yours is a case in point. That holy man with all his virtues looks on all the confusion of the ten thousand things as one. Because of his very existence, the world is emerging from chaos. Why should he do anything about it? Nothing can harm him. A great flood reaching the sky could not drown him. Though a great drought caused metals and rocks to melt and scorched the earth and hills, he would feel no heat. From his own substance he can create philosopher kings like Yao or Shun. Why should he bother with worldly things?"

肩吾問於連叔曰吾聞言於接輿大而無當往而不返吾驚怖其言猶河漢而無極也大有逕庭不近人情焉連叔曰其言謂何哉曰藐姑射之山有神人居焉肌膚若冰雪淖約若處子不食五穀吸風飲露乘雲氣御飛龍而遊乎四海之外其神凝使物不疵癘而年穀熟吾以是狂而不信也連叔曰然瞽者無以與乎文章之觀聾者無以與乎鐘鼓之聲豈唯形骸有聾盲哉夫知亦有之是其言也猶時女也之人也之德也將磅礴萬物以為一世蘄乎亂孰弊弊焉以天下為事之人也物莫之傷大浸稽天而不溺大旱金石流土山焦而不熱是其塵垢粃糠將猶陶鑄堯舜者也孰肯以物為事

宋人資章甫適諸越越人斷髮文身無所用之
堯治天下之民平海內之政往見四子藐姑射之山
汾水之陽窅然喪其天下焉

A man from the state of Sung selling ceremonial caps made a trip to the state of Yueh. But Yueh people, having short hair and tattooed bodies, had no use for them. Yao brought order to the people of the world and ruled wisely over the lands bounded by the four seas. But returning south of the Fen River after his visit to the four sages on Mount Kui, he lost his interest in the empire.

惠子謂莊子曰魏王貽我大瓠之種我樹之成而實五石以盛水漿其堅不能自舉也剖之以為瓢則瓠落無所容非不呺然大也吾為其無用而掊之莊子曰夫子固拙於用大矣宋人有善為不龜手之藥者世世以洴澼絖為事客聞之請買其方百金聚族而謀曰我世世為洴澼絖不過數金今一朝而鬻技百金請與之客得之以說吳王越有難吳王使之將冬與越人水戰大敗越人裂地而封之能不龜手一也或以封或不免於洴澼絖則所用之異也今子有五石之瓠何不慮以為大樽而浮乎江湖而憂其瓠落無所容則夫子猶有蓬之心也夫惠子謂莊子曰吾有大樹人謂之樗其大本擁腫而不中繩墨其小枝卷曲而不中規矩立之塗匠者不顧今子之言大而無用眾所同去也莊子曰子獨不見狸狌乎卑身而伏以候敖者東西跳梁不辟高下中於機辟死於罔罟今夫斄牛其大若垂天之雲此能為大矣而不能執鼠今子有大樹患其無用何不樹之於無何有之鄉廣莫之野彷徨乎無為其側逍遙乎寢臥其下不夭斤斧物無害者

Hui Tsu said to Chuang Tsu, "The King of Wei gave me some seeds from a huge gourd. I planted them and they bore a fruit big enough to hold five bushels. I used it to carry water, but it was too heavy to lift. So I cut it in half to make ladles, but they were too shallow to hold anything. They were big, unwieldy, and useless so I smashed them into pieces."

Chuang Tsu said, "My friend, you are not very intelligent in your use of large things. There was a man from Sung who could make a good salve for chapped hands. His family had had a silk-bleaching business for generations. A traveler heard of this and offered to buy the secret formula for one hundred pieces of gold. The family gathered together to have a conference and said, 'We have been bleaching silk for generations and have earned only a few pieces of gold. Now in one day we can sell the secret for one hundred pieces of gold. Let him have it.'

"The traveler took it and offered it to the King of Wu. Wu and Yueh were at war. The King of Wu entrusted the traveler with the command of his fleet. In the winter the fleet fought a naval battle against Yueh and totally defeated it. The traveler was rewarded with a fief and title.

"In both cases, the cure for chapped hands was the same but was used differently. One man got a title, while the others are still bleaching silk. Now, you had a gourd big enough to hold five bushels. Why didn't you think of making it into a great barrel and using it to float along the rivers and lakes instead of worrying about its being useless for holding anything. Your mind, my friend, is still very cluttered with trivia."

Hui Tsu said, "I have a big ailanthus tree. Its trunk is so gnarled and full of knots that it is impossible to measure it accurately. Its branches are too twisted and crooked for anyone to measure with a compass and square. It stands at the side of the road, but no carpenter would give it a second glance. Now, your words are as big and useless; no one wants to hear what you have to say."

Chuang Tsu replied, "Have you ever watched a wildcat or a weasel? It crouches close to the ground and waits for its prey. Then it leaps up and down, first one way, then the other, until it catches and kills its prey. Then again there is the yak, as great as a cloud shadowing the sky. Big as it is, it cannot catch a mouse. Now, you have this giant tree and are concerned that it is useless. Why don't you plant it on land where nothing grows, in a wild barren place? There you may saunter idly around it, doing nothing, and lie down to sleep beneath its boughs. No one will try to cut it down. Nothing can harm it since it has no use. How can it cause you any anxiety?"

齊物論

CHAPTER TWO

THE EQUALITY
OF ALL THINGS

Nan Kuo Tsu Chi sat leaning on a low table, gazing at the heavens and sighing; he appeared to be in a trance. His disciple Yen Cheng Tsu Yu, who was standing beside him, exclaimed, "What is this? Can you really make your body like dry wood and your mind like dead ashes? The man leaning on the table is not the one who was here a moment ago."

Tsu Chi said, "Yen, it is good that you asked that. Just now I lost myself. Do you understand? Perhaps you have heard the music of man but not the music of earth. You may have heard the music of earth but not the music of heaven."

Tsu Yu said, "May I ask you to say more about this?"

Tsu Chi answered, "The universe has a cosmic breath. Its name is wind. Sometimes it is not active; but when it is, angry howls rise from ten thousand openings. Have you ever heard a roaring gale?

In the mountain forest, deep and fearsome, there are huge trees a hundred arm spans around, with gaps and hollows like nostrils, mouths, and ears, like gouges, goblets, and mortars, and like muddy pools and dirty puddles. The sounds rush out like water, whistle like arrows, scold, suck, shout, wail, moan, and howl. The leading notes are hissing sounds followed by a roaring chorus. Gentle breezes make a small harmony, fierce winds a great one. When the violent gusts subside, all the hollows become quiet. Have you ever seen the shaking and trembling of branches and leaves?"

Tsu Yu said, "The earth's music is the sound from those hollows. Man's music comes from the hollow reed. May I ask about the music of heaven?"

Tsu Chi said, "When the wind blows through the ten thousand different hollows, they all make their own sounds. Why should there be anything else that causes the sound?"

Great knowledge is all-encompassing; small knowledge is limited. Great words are inspiring; small words are chatter. When we are asleep, we are in touch with our souls. When we are awake, our senses open. We get involved with our activities and our minds are distracted. Sometimes we are hesitant, sometimes underhanded, and sometimes secretive. Little fears cause anxiety, and great fears cause panic. Our words fly off like arrows, as though we knew what was right and wrong. We cling to our own point of view, as though everything depended on it. And yet our opinions have no permanence: like autumn and winter, they gradually pass away. We are caught in the current and cannot return. We are tied up in knots like an old clogged drain; we are getting closer to death with no way to regain our youth. Joy and anger, sorrow and happiness, hope and fear, indecision and strength, humility and willfulness, enthusiasm and insolence, like music sounding from an empty reed or mushrooms rising from the warm dark earth, continually appear before us day and night. No one knows whence they come. Don't worry about it! Let them be! How can we understand it all in one day?

If there is no other, there is no I. If there is no I, there is no one to perceive. This is close to the truth, but we do not know why. There must be some primal force, but we cannot discover any proof. I believe it acts, but I cannot see it. I can feel it, but it has no form.

The hundred joints, nine openings, and six organs all function together. Which part do you prefer? Do you like them all equally, or do you have a favorite? Are they not all servants? Can they keep order among themselves, or do they take turns being masters and servants? It may be that there is indeed a true master. Whether I really feel his existence or not has nothing to do with the way it is. Once a man is given a body it works naturally as long as it lasts. It carries on through hardship and ease and, like a galloping horse, nothing can stop it. Isn't it sad? All through life one toils and sweats, never seeing any result. Weary and exhausted, man has no place to rest his bones. Isn't this a pity? One may say, "There is no death." What good does that do? When the body decays, so does the mind. Is this not a great sorrow? Is life really this absurd? Am I the only one who sees the absurdity? Don't others see it too?

If one is true to one's self and follows its teaching, who need be without a teacher? Not only those who are experienced and wise may have a teacher, the fools have theirs too. When those who are not true to themselves try to choose between right and wrong, it is as if they set off for Yueh today and arrived yesterday. That would be making what does not exist,

exist. How do you make what does not exist, exist? Even the holy man Yu did not know how to do this, much less a person like me.

Words are not just blown air. They have a meaning. If you are not sure what you are talking about, are you saying anything, or are you saying nothing? Words seem different from the chirping of birds. Is there a difference, or isn't there? How can Tao be so obscure and yet admit of truth and falsehood? How can words be so obscure and yet admit of right and wrong? How can Tao cease to exist? How can words not be heard?

Tao is hidden by partial understanding. The meaning of words is hidden by flowery rhetoric. This is what causes the dissension between the Confucians and the Mohists. What one says is wrong, the other says is right; and what one says is right, the other says is wrong. If the one is right while the other is wrong, and the other is right while the one is wrong, then the best thing to do is to look beyond right and wrong.

夫道天成心而說之說猶是無師也
若心色心心心即水本有之愚年与有云
夫以求心心當生死當言通越穴著云与
生以無有看無有有無看神通
是不解色言獨見本有都
夫亡死吹や六至百一言一言對未定や
男有六希子未當百六物
忍不知患一無穀言母者辨未天無辨申
道患中陰空身自他
六究中陰空身是死
遠患中行空有六究求有空如有道隨於邪有陰求于茫茫
均有儒墨之是非以先死私死空死则生飲先業失聊死
空无衛起見其若以死

Every thing can be a "that"; every thing
can be a "this." One man cannot see
things as another sees them. One can
only know things through knowing oneself. Therefore it is said, " 'That' comes
from 'this,' and 'this' comes from 'that' "
—which means "that" and "this"
give birth to one another. Life arises
from death and death from life. What
is inappropriate is seen by virtue of
what is appropriate. There is right because of wrong, and wrong because of
right. Thus, the sage does not bother
with these distinctions but seeks enlight-
enment from heaven. So he sees "this,"
but "this" is also "that," and "that" is
also "this." "That" has elements of right
and wrong, and "this" has elements of
right and wrong. Does he still distinguish
between "this" and "that," or doesn't
he? When there is no more separation between "this" and "that," it is called the
still-point of Tao. At the still-point in
the center of the circle one can see the infinite in all things. Right is infinite; wrong
is also infinite. Therefore it is said, "Be-
hold the light beyond right and wrong."

To use one's fingers to demonstrate fingers not being fingers is not as good as using something else to demonstrate fingers not being fingers. Using horses to demonstrate horses not being horses is not as good as using something else to demonstrate horses not being horses. "Heaven and earth" are like a finger; "the ten thousand things" are like a horse.

What is acceptable is acceptable; what is not acceptable is not acceptable. A path is formed by walking on it. A thing has a name because of its being called something. Why is it like this? Because it is! Why is it not like that? Because it is not! Everything has its own nature and its own function. Nothing is without nature or function. Consider a small stalk or a great column, a leper or a beauty, things that are great or wicked, perverse, and strange. They are all one in Tao.

When there is separation, there is coming together. When there is coming together, there is dissolution. All things may become one, whatever their state of being. Only he who has transcended sees this oneness. He has no use for differences and dwells in the constant. To be constant is to be useful. To be useful is to realize one's true nature. Realization of one's true nature is happiness. When one reaches happiness, one is close to perfection. So one stops, yet does not know that one stops. This is Tao.

When you wrack your brain trying to unify things without knowing that they are already one, it is called "three in the morning." What do I mean by "three in the morning"? A man who kept monkeys said to them, "You get three acorns in the morning and four in the evening." This made them all very angry. So he said, "How about four in the morning and three in the evening?"—and the monkeys were happy. The number of acorns was the same, but the different arrangement resulted in anger or pleasure. This is what I am talking about. Therefore, the sage harmonizes right with wrong and rests in the balance of nature. This is called taking both sides at once.

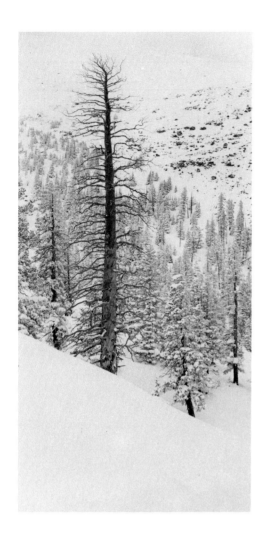

When there is rise and fall, Chao Wen plays the lute. When there is no rise and fall, Chao Wen does not play the lute.

Chao Wen played the lute, Shia Kuang kept time with a baton, and Hui Tsu leaned on a stump and debated. Each of these three masters was nearly perfect in his own art. Their names will be remembered forevermore. Because they excelled, they were distinguished from others. Because they excelled, they wanted to enlighten others through their art. They tried to teach what could not be taught. This resulted in obscure discussions as to the nature of "hardness" and "whiteness." Their sons followed in their fathers' footsteps all their lives but accomplished nothing. However, if this can be called accomplishment, then even I have accomplished something. If this cannot be called accomplishment, then neither I nor others have accomplished anything. Therefore, the sage seeks insight from chaos and doubt. Not making distinctions but dwelling on that which is unchanging is called clear vision.

Among the ancients, knowledge was very deep. What is meant by deep? It reached back to the time when nothing existed. It was so deep, so complete, that nothing could be added to it. Then came men who distinguished between things but did not give them names. Later they labeled them but did not choose between right and wrong. When right and wrong appeared, Tao declined. With the fall of Tao, desire arose. Is there really rise and fall?

Now I am going to tell you something. I don't know what heading it comes under, and whether or not it is relevant here, but it must be relevant at some point. It is not anything new, but I would like to say it.

There is a beginning. There is no beginning of that beginning. There is no beginning of that no beginning of beginning. There is something. There is nothing. There is something before the beginning of something and nothing, and something before that. Suddenly there is something and nothing. But between something and nothing, I still don't really know which is something and which is nothing. Now, I've just said something, but I don't really know whether I've said anything or not.

There is nothing in the world greater than the tip of a bird's feather, and Mount Tai is small. None have lived longer than a dead child, and old Peng Tsu died young. Heaven and earth grow together with me, and the ten thousand things and I are one. We are already one— what else is there to say? Yet I have just said that we are one, so my words exist also. The one and what I said about the one make two, and two and one make three. Thus it goes on and on. Even a skilled mathematician cannot reach the end, much less an ordinary man. If we proceed from nothing to something, we reach three. How much farther would it be going from something to something? Enough. Let us stop.

夫道未始有封，言未始有常，為是而有畛也。請言其畛：有左，有右，有倫，有義，有分，有辯，有競，有爭，此之謂八德。六合之外，聖人存而不論；六合之內，聖人論而不議。春秋經世先王之志，聖人議而不辯。故分也者，有不分也；辯也者，有不辯也。曰：何也？聖人懷之，眾人辯之以相示也。故曰辯也者有不見也。

At first Tao had no name. Words are not eternal. Because of words, there are distinctions. Let me describe these distinctions. There is left, and there is right; there is relationship, and there is duty; there is discernment, and there is discrimination; there is competition, and there is struggle. These are called the eight virtues.

Beyond the six realms of heaven, earth, and the four directions, the sage accepts but does not discuss. Within the six realms, he discusses but does not pass judgment. In the Book of Spring and Autumn, the chronicle of the ancient kings, the sage passes judgment but does not question. When there is division, there is something which is not divided. When there is questioning, there is something beyond the question. Why is this? The sage keeps his wisdom to himself while ordinary men flaunt their knowledge in loud discussion. So I say, "Those who dispute do not see."

Great Tao is beyond description. Great argument uses no words. Great goodness is not kind. Great integrity is not incorruptible. Great courage is not aggressive. Tao that is manifest is not Tao. Words that argue miss the point. Perpetual kindness does not work. Obvious integrity is not believed. Aggressive courage will not win. These five are round and mellow, yet they may become square and inflexible.

Knowing enough to stop when one does not know is perfection.

Who can understand an argument that has no words and Tao that cannot be expressed? If a man can understand this, then he may be called the treasure house of heaven. Pour into it, and it will never be filled; pour out of it, and it will never be emptied. Yet no one knows why this is so. This is called the hidden light.

Long ago, Emperor Yao said to Shun, "I would like to attack the states of Tsung, Kuei, and Hsu Ao. This has been on my mind ever since I came to the throne. Why is this so?"

Shun said, "These three states eke out their existence in the weeds and bushes. Why bother? There was a time when ten suns rose all at once and the ten thousand things were illuminated. And yet how much greater is virtue than these suns!"

夫大道不称大辩不言大仁不仁大廉不嗛大勇不忮道昭而不道言辩而不及仁常而不成廉清而不信勇忮而不成五者园而几向方矣故知止其所不知至矣孰知不言之辩不道之道若有能知此之谓天府注焉而不满酌焉而不竭而不知其所由来此之谓葆光故昔者尧问于舜曰我欲伐宗脍胥敖南面而不释然其故何也舜曰夫三子者犹存乎蓬艾之间若不释然何哉昔者十日并出万物皆照而况德之进乎日者乎

Yeh Chueh asked Wang I, "Do you know what is common to all things?"

"How should I know?" he replied.

"Do you know that you don't know?"

"How should I know?" he replied again.

"Then are all things not knowable?"

"How should I know? Still, let me put it this way: How do you know that what I say I know may not really be what I don't know? How do you know that what I say I don't know may not really be what I know? Now let me ask you something. If a man sleeps in a damp place, his back will ache and he will be half paralyzed. But does this happen to eels? If a man lives up in a tree, he will tremble with fright. But does this happen to monkeys? Of these three, who knows the right place to live? Men eat flesh, deer eat grass, centipedes delight in worms, and owls and crows like mice. Of these four, which know what to eat? Monkeys mate with monkeys. Elk and deer run together, and eels play with fish.

"Mao Chiang and Li Chi were considered beautiful by men. But if fish saw them, they would dive to the bottom of the river. If birds saw them, they would fly off. If deer saw them, they would run away. Of these four, who recognizes real beauty?

"As I see it, the rules of goodness and wisdom and the paths of right and wrong are inextricably mingled and confused. How can I tell which is which?"

Yeh Chueh asked, "If you cannot distinguish between good and evil, then can the perfect man distinguish between them?"

Wang I replied, "The perfect man is spiritual. Though the great swamp burns, he will not feel the heat. Though the great rivers freeze, he will not feel the cold. Though thunderbolts split the mountains and gales shake the sea, he will have no fear. Such a man can ride the clouds and mist, mount the sun and moon, and wander beyond the four seas. Life and death do not affect him. How much less will he be concerned with good and evil!"

Chu Chiao Tsu asked Chang Wu Tsu, "I have heard from Confucius that the sage is not troubled by worldly things. He does not look for gain or try to avoid loss; he seeks nothing, and does not cling to Tao. Sometimes he says something without words, and sometimes his words say nothing. Thus he travels beyond the dusty world. Confucius thought these words to be mere fantasy. But I think this is the way of the unfathomable Tao. What do you think?"

Chang Wu Tsu replied, "These words would have confused even the Yellow Emperor, so how could Confucius understand them? Moreover, you are too quick to draw conclusions. You see an egg, and immediately you listen for the crowing of a full-grown cock. You see a bow, and you look for a roast dove. Let me give you a rough explanation, but don't take this too literally. All right? How could anyone take his place beside the sun and moon, embrace the universe, be at one with all, refrain from interfering, and disregard the social order? Ordinary men labor and toil. The sage acts without choosing. He experiences ten thousand years as one age. To him the ten thousand things are what they are, yet they form a whole."

瞿鵲子問於長梧子曰、吾聞諸夫子、
聖人不從事於務、不就利、不違害、不喜求、
不緣道、有謂無謂、無謂有謂、而遊乎塵垢之外。夫子以為
孟浪之言、而我以為妙道之行也。吾子以為奚若。
長梧子曰、是黃帝之所聽熒也、而丘
也何足以知之。且女亦大早計、
見卵而求時夜、見彈而求鴞炙。
予嘗為女妄言之、女以妄聽之。
奚旁日月、挾宇宙、為其脗合、
置其滑涽、以隸相尊。眾人役役、聖人愚芚、
參萬歲而一成純。
萬物盡然、而以是相蘊。

予惡乎知說生之非惑邪！予惡乎知惡死之非弱喪而不知歸者邪！麗之姬，艾封人之子也。晉國之始得之也，涕泣沾襟；及其至於王所，與王同筐床，食芻豢，而後悔其泣也。予惡乎知夫死者不悔其始之蘄生乎！夢飲酒者，旦而哭泣；夢哭泣者，旦而田獵。方其夢也，不知其夢也。夢之中又占其夢焉，覺而後知其夢也。且有大覺而後知此其大夢也，而愚者自以為覺，竊竊然知之。君乎，牧乎，固哉！丘也與女，皆夢也；予謂女夢，亦夢也。是其言也，其名為弔詭。萬世之後而一遇大聖，知其解者，是旦暮遇之也。

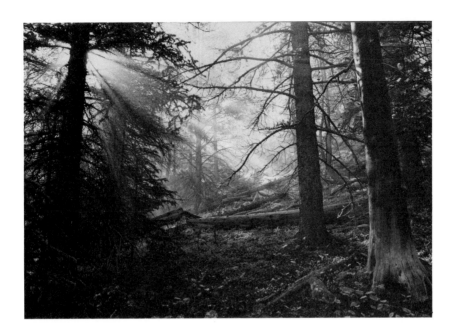

"How can I tell if love of life is not a delusion? How can I tell whether a man who fears death is not like a man who has left home and dreads returning? Lady Li was the daughter of a border guard of Ai. When the Duke of Chin first took her captive, she wept until her dress was soaked with tears. But once she was living in the Duke's palace, sharing his bed, and eating delicious food, she wondered why she had ever cried. How can I tell whether the dead are not amazed that they ever clung to life?

"Those who dream of a great feast may weep the next morning. Those who dream of weeping may enjoy the hunt the next day. While they dream, they do not know they are dreaming. They may even interpret their dreams while still dreaming. Only after they awake do they know it was a dream. By and by, there will be a great awakening; then we will know that this is all a great dream. All the while, the fools think they are awake, appearing to understand things, calling this man ruler and that man herdsman. How stupid! You and Confucius are both dreaming. When I say you are dreaming, I am dreaming too. These words may sound like double-talk. Yet after ten thousand generations, we will meet a great sage who can explain all this. Or it may happen any time now."

Suppose you and I argue. If you win and I lose, are you indeed right and I wrong? And if I win and you lose, am I right and you wrong? Are we both partly right and partly wrong? Are we both all right or both all wrong? If you and I cannot see the truth, other people will find it even harder.

Then whom shall I ask to be the judge? Shall I ask someone who agrees with you? If he already agrees with you, how can he be a fair judge? Shall I ask someone who agrees with me? If he already agrees with me, how can he be a fair judge? Shall I ask someone who agrees with both of us? If he already agrees with both of us, how can he be a fair judge? Then if you and I and others cannot decide, shall we wait for still another? Waiting for changing opinions is like waiting for nothing. Seeing everything in relation to the heavenly cosmos and leaving the different viewpoints as they are, we may be able to live out our years.

What do I mean by seeing things in relation to the heavenly cosmos? Consider right and wrong, being and non-being. If right is indeed right, there need be no argument about how it is different from wrong. If being is really being, there need be no argument about how it is different from non-being. Forget time; forget distinction. Enjoy the infinite; rest in it.

既使我與若辯矣若勝我我不若勝若果是也
我果非也邪我勝若若不我勝我果是也而果非也邪
其或是也邪其或非也邪其俱是也邪其俱非也邪
我與若不能相知也則人固受其黮闇吾誰使正之
使同乎若者正之既與若同矣惡能正之
使同乎我者正之既同乎我矣惡能正之
使異乎我與若者正之既異乎我與若矣惡能正之
使同乎我與若者正之既同乎我與若矣惡能正之
然則我與若與人俱不能相知也而待彼也邪
化聲之相待若其不相待和之以天倪因之以曼衍所以窮年也
何謂和之以天倪曰是不是然不然
是若果是也則是之異乎不是也亦無辯
然若果然也則然之異乎不然也亦無辯
忘年忘義振於無竟故寓諸無竟

Shade said to Shadow, "A little while ago, you were moving; and now you are standing still. A little while ago, you were sitting down; and now you are getting up. Why all this indecision?"

Shadow replied, "Don't I have to depend on others to be what I am? Don't others also have to depend on something else to be what they are? My dependence is like that of the snake on his skin or of the cicada on his wings. How can I tell why I do this, or why I do that?"

Once upon a time, I, Chuang Tsu, dreamed I was a butterfly flying happily here and there, enjoying life without knowing who I was. Suddenly I woke up and I was indeed Chuang Tsu. Did Chuang Tsu dream he was a butterfly, or did the butterfly dream he was Chuang Tsu? There must be some distinction between Chuang Tsu and the butterfly. This is a case of transformation.

罔兩問景曰曩子行今子止曩子坐今子起何其無特操與
景曰吾有待而然者邪吾所待又有待而然者邪吾待蛇蚹蜩翼邪惡識所以然惡識所以不然
昔者莊周夢為胡蝶栩栩然胡蝶也自喻適志與不知周也俄然覺則蘧蘧然周也不知周之夢為胡蝶與胡蝶之夢為周與周與胡蝶則必有分矣此之謂物化

CHAPTER THREE

THE SECRET
OF GROWTH

吾生也有涯而知也无涯
以有涯随无涯殆已
已而知为殆而已矣
为善无近名为恶无近刑
缘督以为经可以保身可以
可以养亲可以尽年

Life has a limit, but knowledge is without limit. For the limited to pursue the unlimited is futile. To know this and still pursue knowledge is even more futile. In doing good, avoid fame. In doing evil, avoid punishment. Thus, by pursuing the middle way, you may preserve your body, fulfill your life, look after your parents, and live out your years.

庖丁為文惠君解牛、手之所觸、肩之所
倚、足之所履、膝之所踦、砉然嚮然、奏刀騞然、莫不中音、
合於桑林之舞、乃中經首之會、文惠君曰、譆善哉
技蓋至此乎、庖丁釋刀對曰、臣之所好者
進乎技矣、始臣之解牛之時、所見無非牛者、
三年之後、未嘗見全牛也、方今之時、臣以神遇、
而不以目視、官知止而神欲行、依乎天理、
批大郤、導大窾、因其固然、技經肯綮之未嘗、
而況大軱乎、良庖歲更刀、割也、族庖月更刀折也、
今臣之刀十九年矣、所解數千牛矣、而
刀刃若新發於硎、彼節者有間、而刀刃者無厚、
以無厚入有間、恢恢乎其於遊刃必有餘地矣、
是以十九年而刀刃若新發於硎、雖然、每至於族、
吾見其難為、怵然為戒、視為止、行為遲、動刀甚微、
謋然已解、如土委地、提刀而立、為之四顧、為之
躊躇滿志、善刀而藏之、君曰、善哉、吾聞庖丁之言、得養生焉
写

Prince Wen Hui's cook was carving up an ox. Every touch of his hand, every heave of his shoulder, every step of his foot, every thrust of his knee, with the slicing and parting of the flesh, and the zinging of the knife—all was in perfect rhythm, just like the Dance of the Mulberry Grove or a part in the Ching Shou symphony.

Prince Wen Hui remarked, "How wonderfully you have mastered your art."

The cook laid down his knife and said, "What your servant really cares for is Tao, which goes beyond mere art. When I first began to cut up oxen, I saw nothing but oxen. After three years of practicing, I no longer saw the ox as a whole. I now work with my spirit, not with my eyes. My senses stop functioning and my spirit takes over. I follow the natural grain, letting the knife find its way through the many hidden openings, taking advantage of what is there, never touching a ligament or tendon, much less a main joint.

"A good cook changes his knife once a year because he cuts, while a mediocre cook has to change his every month because he hacks. I've had this knife of mine for nineteen years and have cut up thousands of oxen with it, and yet the edge is as if it were fresh from the grindstone. There are spaces between the joints. The blade of the knife has no thickness. That which has no thickness has plenty of room to pass through these spaces. Therefore, after nineteen years, my blade is as sharp as ever. However, when I come to a difficulty, I size up the joint, look carefully, keep my eyes on what I am doing, and work slowly. Then with a very slight movement of the knife, I cut the whole ox wide open. It falls apart like a clod of earth crumbling to the ground. I stand there with the knife in my hand, looking about me with a feeling of accomplishment and delight. Then I wipe the knife clean and put it away."

"Well done!" said the Prince. "From the words of my cook, I have learned the secret of growth."

公み叩見右師〜噂々日是月の人や悲帝合心天ら々こ人ら々日天や知人や
天之先を是供独や人之豹有ら々以是を天天や知人や
潅雄十牛一咏る年一飲不斬音字樊中神亀を不善や

When Kung Wen Hsien saw the Commander of the Army, he was startled and
exclaimed, "Who is this? Why does he
have only one foot? Was it the work of
heaven or of man?" The Commander
said, "It was the work of heaven, not man.
Heaven made me one-footed. Heaven de-
termines man's appearance; therefore I
know it was heaven, not man. The pheas-
ant in the marshes has to take ten steps
in order to get one beakful of food, one
hundred steps for one drink of water. Yet
it doesn't want to be kept in a cage.
Though it would be fed like a king, it
would not be happy."

When Lao Tsu died, Chin Shih went to the funeral. He yelled three times and left.

A disciple said, "Were you not a friend of the Master?"

"Yes."

"Then is it proper to mourn him in this way?"

"Yes. When I first arrived, I thought his spirit was really there. Now I know it wasn't. When I went in to mourn, the old people were wailing as though they had lost their son. The young ones were crying as though they had lost their mother. Since they were all together, they talked and wept without any control. This is avoiding heaven, indulging in sentiment, ignoring what is natural. In the old days, it was called the crime of violating the law of nature.

"The Master came because it was time. He left because he followed the natural flow. Be content with the moment, and be willing to follow the flow; then there will be no room for grief or joy. In the old days this was called freedom from bondage. The wood is consumed but the fire burns on, and we do not know when it will come to an end."

人間は

CHAPTER FOUR

HUMAN AFFAIRS

Yen Hui went to Confucius to say goodbye.

The Master asked, "Where are you going?"

"I am going to Wei."

"What are you going to do there?"

"I hear that the Prince of Wei is young and that he is arbitrary in his actions. He is not much concerned with his country and is not aware of his mistakes. He thinks nothing of people dying. The dead lie everywhere like thick grass in a swamp.

The people have nowhere to turn. I've heard you, Master, say, 'Leave the country that is already well governed and go to a country that is in chaos.' At the door of a physician, there are many sick people. I would like to use your teaching to remedy the situation there."

Confucius said, "Ah! If you go there, you will only get into trouble. Tao must be pure. When something is added to it, there is confusion. When there is confusion, there is anxiety. With anxiety, there is no hope. The wise men of old realized Tao in themselves before they offered it to others. If you are not certain that you have it in yourself, how can you change a tyrant's action?

"Besides, do you know how virtue degenerates and how learning arises? Virtue is consumed by fame. Learning is born of contention. Fame causes men to fight with one another. Learning is the weapon for the struggle. Both can be evil instruments. They are not the means to perfection. Though you are highly virtuous and trustworthy, if you do not understand the spirit of men, and though you are famous and do not compete, if you do not understand the minds of men, but instead go to a tyrant and lecture him on goodness, ethical behavior, measures and standards, you are just using the failings of others to demonstrate your own superiority. This is deliberately hurting other people. One who hurts others will in turn be hurt. You will probably end up in trouble."

顔回見仲尼請行曰奚之曰將之衛曰奚為焉曰回聞衛君其年壯其行獨輕用其國而不見其過輕用民死死者以國量乎澤若蕉民其無如矣回嘗聞之夫子曰治國去之亂國就之醫門多疾願以所聞思其則庶幾其國有瘳乎仲尼曰譆若殆往而刑耳夫道不欲雜雜則多多則擾擾則憂憂而不救古之至人先存諸己而後存諸人所存於己者未定何暇至於暴人之所行且若亦知夫德之所蕩而知之所為出乎哉德蕩乎名知出乎爭名也者相軋也知也者爭之器也二者凶器非所以盡行也且德厚信矼未達人氣名聞不爭未達人心而強以仁義繩墨之言術暴人之前者是以人惡有其美也命之曰菑人菑人者人必反菑之若殆為人菑夫

其苗尚悦賢而悪不肖悪用而求有以異若喩
而目得榮之而色逆将平之口将営之以形
沈溺水名之曰過多順此夫宗苦弱必以不信厚言必死死暴人之将美
目者本築殺闘庵筆封殺王子比干是修夫身以下慮拊人之氏
以下撩夫舂也故夫君困於修以擁之是好名本也者本美之叢枝是敢
惡玲有庵困百霊勇而形戴其用兵必以上来宴無己是以求名実者也
而独不聞之平名実聖人之所不能脱也而況若乎然若必有以
赏以語弟来

"If indeed the Prince likes good men and hates bad men, why would you try to change him? If he does not, you would be better off saying nothing; for if you do speak, the Prince will expose your weak points and win the argument. You will look confused and ashamed; you will find one excuse after another and you will seem to yield. Your mind will be molded to his way of thinking. This is putting out fire with fire, adding water to a flood; it is called adding to the excess. If you start by giving in, there will be no end to your concessions. And if you speak out strongly against him, he will not listen to you and will undoubtedly put you to death.

"In ancient times, Chieh killed Kuan Lung Pang and Chou killed Prince Pi Kan. These two victims were virtuous men who tried hard to comfort and aid the common people. In this way they offended their superiors. Their rulers had them put to death because of their goodness. This was the result of seeking fame for their virtue. Many years ago, Yao attacked the states of Tsung Chi and Hsu Ao; Yu attacked Yuo Hu. These nations were laid waste and destroyed, their rulers killed. For all of them were constantly at war in an effort to win more. They were all seekers of fame and wealth. Have you never heard of them? Even wise men cannot deal with fame and wealth. So how can you? However, you must have something else in mind. Come tell me what it is."

Yen Hui said, "If I am detached and self-assured, persevering and of one mind, won't that work?"

"What! How can that work? You may put on a brave show, but your uncertainty will appear on your face as it would with anyone else. This prince takes pleasure in exploiting the feelings of others. He cannot even practice the ordinary virtues. How do you expect him to appreciate the higher virtues? He will be obstinate and unbending. Outwardly he may agree, but there will be no inward change of heart. How can you succeed in that way?"

"Well then, I will be inwardly firm and outwardly compliant. I will arm myself with examples from antiquity. Being inwardly firm, I will be a follower of heaven. Being a follower of heaven, I know that the Prince and I are both sons of heaven. So, why should I mind whether or not people approve of my words? People call this being childlike. This is what I call being a follower of heaven.

"By being outwardly compliant, I am a follower of men. Lifting the tablet, kneeling, bending, and bowing—this is how a minister behaves. All men do this. Why shouldn't I? Do as others do, and there is no trouble! This is what I call being a follower of men.

"By observing the customs, I will be following ancient tradition. Though my words may be chiding and critical, they will not be my own words but the words of the sages. So I need not be afraid of speaking out. This is what I mean by following tradition. Will that work?"

Confucius said, "How could that work? You have too many plans. They are fine but not appropriate. These preconceived ideas probably won't get you into trouble, but that is as far as they go. How can you possibly influence him? You are still too rigid in your thinking."

Yen Hui said, "That is all I can think of. May I ask what to do?"

Confucius said, "You must fast. I'll tell you why. Is it easy to work from preconceived ideas? Heaven frowns on those who think it is easy."

Yen Hui said, "My family is poor. I have neither drunk wine nor eaten meat for many months. Can this be considered fasting?"

Confucius replied, "That is the fasting one does for sacrificial ceremonies, not the fasting of the mind."

Yen Hui said, "May I ask what is fasting of the mind?"

Confucius said, "Your will must be one. Do not listen with your ears but with your mind. Do not listen with your mind but with your vital energy. Ears can only hear, mind can only think, but vital energy is empty, receptive to all things. Tao abides in emptiness. Emptiness is the fasting of mind."

Yen Hui said, "Before I heard all this, I was certain that I was Hui. Now that I've heard it, I am no longer Hui. Can this be called emptiness?"

Confucius said, "That is it. Let me explain. You can enter this man's service, but do not thrust yourself forward. If he listens, then speak. If not, be silent. Leave no opening, and you will not be harmed. Be always at one and accept whatever happens. Then you are close to success. If you do not move, then it is easy to remain unnoticed. But it is hard to walk without touching the ground. It is easy to be a hypocrite in your dealings with men. It is hard to be a hypocrite in your dealings with heaven.

"You understand how to fly using wings, but you have not yet seen how to fly without them. You understand how to act from knowledge, but you have not yet seen how to act from not-knowing. Look at empty space. It is in emptiness that light is born. There is happiness in stillness. Lack of stillness is called sitting while wandering. If you are open to everything you see and hear, and allow this to act through you, even gods and spirits will come to you, not to speak of men. This is the transformation of the ten thousand things, the secret of the wise kings Yu and Shun, the constant practice of Fu Hsi and Chi Chu. It is even more useful for ordinary men."

顏回曰：「吾無以進矣，敢問其方。」仲尼曰：「齋，吾將語若！有而為之，其易邪？易之者，暤天不宜。」顏回曰：「回之家貧，唯不飲酒不茹葷者數月矣。如此，則可以為齋乎？」曰：「是祭祀之齋，非心齋也。」回曰：「敢問心齋。」仲尼曰：「若一志，無聽之以耳而聽之以心，無聽之以心而聽之以氣！聽止於耳，心止於符。氣也者，虛而待物者也。唯道集虛。虛者，心齋也。」

顏回曰：「回之未始得使，實自回也；得使之也，未始有回也；可謂虛乎？」夫子曰：「盡矣。吾語若！若能入遊其樊而無感其名，入則鳴，不入則止。無門無毒，一宅而寓於不得已，則幾矣。絕跡易，無行地難。為人使易以偽，為天使難以偽。聞以有翼飛者矣，未聞以無翼飛者也；聞以有知知者矣，未聞以無知知者也。瞻彼闋者，虛室生白，吉祥止止。夫且不止，是之謂坐馳。夫徇耳目內通而外於心知，鬼神將來舍，而況人乎！是萬物之化也，禹舜之所紐也，伏戲、几蘧之所行終，而況散焉者乎！」

Tsu Kao, the Duke of She, was being sent to the state of Chi on a mission, and went first to consult Confucius, saying, "The King is dispatching me on a very important mission. Chi will probably treat me with great respect but will be slow to start our discussions. Even an ordinary man is not easily hurried, much less a feudal lord. I am very worried. You always said to me, 'In all matters, great or small, few will succeed without following Tao.' If this mission is not successful, I shall be criticized. If it is successful, I will be troubled by confusion and anxiety. Only a wise man is not concerned with results—and is therefore unaffected by the outcome. I eat simple unspiced food, so I never need cooling drinks. I received these orders one morning, and by the evening I was drinking vast quantities of water. Am I not feverish? I have not yet seen the actual situation and already I am troubled by anxiety and confusion. If I do not succeed, I am bound to be criticized. I am in a double bind. This is beyond my capacity as a minister. Will you tell me what to do?"

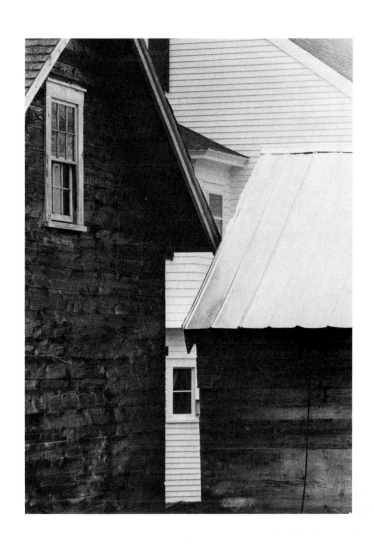

葉子高將使於齊問於仲尼曰王使諸梁也甚重齊之待使不甚敬而急之患莫若於此吾未至而心甚熱矣吾食也執粗而不臧爨無欲清之人今吾朝受命而夕飲冰我其內熱與吾未得事之實而既有陰陽之患矣事若不成必有人道之患是兩也為人臣者不足以任之子其有以語我來仲尼曰天下有大戒二其一命也其一義也子之愛親命也不可解於心臣之事君義也無適而非君也無所逃於天地之間是之謂大戒是以夫事其親者不擇地而安之孝之至也夫事其君者不擇事而安之忠之盛也自事其心者哀樂不易施乎前知其不可奈何而安之若命德之至也為人臣子者固有所不得已行事之情而忘其身何暇至於悅生而惡死夫子其行可矣

仲尼曰天下有大戒二其一命也其一義也子之愛親命也

不可解於心臣之事君義也無適而非君也無所逃於天地之間

是之謂大戒是以夫事其親者不擇地而安之孝之至也

夫事其君者不擇事而安之忠之盛也自事其心者

哀樂不易施乎前知其不可奈何而安之若命德之至也

為人臣子者固有所不得已行事之情而忘其身何暇

至於悦生而惡死夫子其行可矣丘請復以所聞

凡交近則必相靡以信遠則必忠之以言言必或傳之

夫傳兩喜兩怒之言天下之難者也夫兩喜必多溢美之言

兩怒必多溢惡之言凡溢之類妄妄則其信之也莫

莫則傳言者殃故法言曰傳其常情無傳其溢言則幾乎全

Confucius replied, "In the affairs of the world, two universal principles may be observed: one is the natural order and the other is duty. It is natural for a son to love his parents; this cannot be erased from his heart. It is duty for a man to serve his sovereign; everywhere he goes there will be a sovereign. Within heaven and earth, there is no escape. That is why they are called universal principles. Therefore, to honor one's parents, wherever one may be, is the fullness of devotion. To serve one's sovereign willingly, whatever happens, is the perfect loyalty. To serve one's own mind, unmoved by sadness or joy, accepting whatever happens, is the true virtue. Being a son or a subject, there is always something unavoidable that one has to do. Do what has to be done and give no thought to yourself; then you will not have time to think about loving life and hating death. Continue in this way and all will go well.

"Let me tell you something else I have heard. If states have close ties, their mutual trust is demonstrated by deeds. If they are far apart, their good faith has to be renewed with words in the form of messages. But carrying messages of delight or anger between two parties is the most difficult thing in the world. When they are both pleased, there is bound to be exaggeration of flattery; when they are both angry, there is bound to be exaggeration of criticism. Exaggeration leads away from truth. Without truth, there will be no trust. When there is no trust, the messengers will be in danger. Therefore, it is said, 'Speak the truth and do not exaggerate; then you will not be harmed.'"

"Moreover, when wrestlers pit their strength against each other, they begin in a lighthearted, open frame of mind but they usually end up looking angry. At the height of the contest, many crafty tricks are played. When men drink during ceremonies, they start off in an orderly manner and usually finish in disarray. At the height of the party, fun becomes chaos. So it is with all things. They begin in good faith and end up in meanness. What was simple in the beginning becomes grotesque in the end. Words are like the wind and the waves; action involves the risk of gain or loss. The wind and the waves are easily set in motion; risk can easily turn into real danger. Hence, anger comes from nothing more than clever words and half-truths. When animals face death, they do not care what noises they make. They growl fiercely and snarl, and then they attack. In the same way, if a man is pushed too far, he turns and strikes without knowing why. If he does not know why, who knows where it will lead? Therefore, it is said, 'Neither deviate from your instructions, nor hurry to finish.' Do not force things. It is dangerous to deviate from instructions or push for completion. It takes a long time to do a thing properly. Once you do something wrong, it may be too late to change it. Can you afford to be careless?

"So then, flow with whatever may happen and let your mind be free; stay centered by accepting whatever you are doing. This is the ultimate. How else can you carry out your task? It is best to leave everything to work naturally, though this is not easy."

且以勇力奮於揚常卒中陰大王剣多弖弖
以乱飲泥丑将中陰常卒中乱大王剣多弖朱凡乙点然
将中添常卒中卿朱作治将簡丁将畢や必臣夫言弖
風波や行在実喪也風波烏以勧初実喪易烏以君
故怒没無由弖言倆古辞獣欵不揮音氣息弗然
加昌乙弖心腐刻核大王則必有不肖忘死之罪不知弖然
苟乃る弖知王然や熟親弖所強を坊其言日大王迷今无功同
過度盡や當弖令功同弱乙弖甚乃左久
悪以及好々弖塘弖中
亞来軸以遊に沈わゆ点弖中
王吴何作団板に沈る也波命
牛天嬉も
※其苗若石波命

顏闔將傅衛靈公太子，而問於蘧伯玉曰：有人於此，其德天殺。與之為無方，則危吾國；與之為有方，則危吾身。其知適足以知人之過，而不知其所以過。若然者，吾奈之何？

蘧伯玉曰：善哉問乎！戒之慎之，正汝身哉！形莫若就，心莫若和。雖然，之二者有患。就不欲入，和不欲出。形就而入，且為顛為滅，為崩為蹶。心和而出，且為聲為名，為妖為孽。

彼且為嬰兒，亦與之為嬰兒；彼且為無町畦，亦與之為無町畦；彼且為無崖，亦與之為無崖，達之入於無疵。

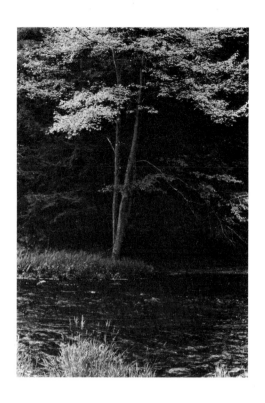

Yen Ho was about to become tutor of the Crown Prince, the son of Duke Ling of the state of Wei. He went to consult Chu Po Yu, saying, "Here is someone who is naturally violent. If I let him remain undisciplined, the state will be in danger. If I try to correct him, I shall endanger myself. He knows enough to see the faults of others, but not to see his own. Under these circumstances, what shall I do?"

Chu Po Yu replied, "That is a good question! Be on guard, be careful, and be sure that you yourself are acting appropriately. Appear to be flexible but maintain harmony within. However, there is danger in doing these two things. While being flexible, be sure to remain centered.

While maintaining harmony within, do not display it openly. If you are too flexible and lose your center, then you will be overcome and destroyed, and you will collapse. If you try to demonstrate your composure, you will be criticized and slandered, called a devil and a son of a bitch. If he wants to be a child, be a child with him. If he wants to act strangely, act strangely with him. If he wants to be reckless, be reckless with him. Then you can reach him and bring him back to his senses."

"Do you know the story of the praying mantis? It raised its arm to stop an approaching carriage unaware that this was beyond its power. Such was its high opinion of itself. Watch out and be careful. If you offend the Prince by showing off your own talents, you court disaster.

"Do you know how a tiger trainer works? He does not risk feeding the tigers live animals for fear of arousing their ferocity as they kill. He does not risk feeding them whole animals for fear of arousing their anger as they tear them apart. He knows when the tigers are hungry and when they are full; thereby he is in touch with their fierce nature. Tigers are a different species from men, yet by observing their ways, one can train them to be gentle. They will kill only when aroused.

"A man with a passion for horses catches the manure in a basket and the piss in a jar. If a mosquito or a fly lands on the horse and he brushes it off too abruptly, then the horse will break its bit, hurt the man's head, and crack his ribs. Such a man has good intentions, but he overdoes it. Can you afford to be careless?"

汝不知夫螳螂乎怒其臂以当車轍不知其不勝任也是其才之美者也
戒之慎之積伐而美者以犯之幾矣
汝不知夫養虎者乎不敢以生物与之為其殺之之怒也
不敢以全物与之
為其決之之怒也時其飢飽達其怒心
虎之与人異類而媚養己者順也
故其殺者逆也
夫愛馬者以筐盛矢以蜄盛溺
適有蚊虻僕緣而拊之不時則缺銜毀首碎胸
意有所至而愛有所亡可不慎邪

Shih the carpenter was on his way to the state of Chi. When he got to Chu Yuan, he saw an oak tree by the village shrine. The tree was large enough to shade several thousand oxen and was a hundred spans around. It towered above the hilltops with its lowest branches eighty feet from the ground. More than ten of its branches were big enough to be made into boats. There were crowds of people as in a marketplace. The master carpenter did not even turn his head but walked on without stopping.

His apprentice took a long look, then ran after Shih the carpenter and said, "Since I took up my ax and followed you, master, I have never seen timber as beautiful as this. But you do not even bother to look at it and walk on without stopping. Why is this?"

Shih the carpenter replied, "Stop! Say no more! That tree is useless. A boat made from it would sink, a coffin would soon rot, a tool would split, a door would ooze sap, and a beam would have termites. It is worthless timber and is of no use. That is why it has reached such a ripe old age."

匠石之齊至乎曲轅
見櫟社樹其大蔽數千牛
絜之百圍其高臨山十仞而後有枝
其可以為舟者旁十數觀
者如市匠伯不顧遂行不輟
弟子厭觀之走及匠石曰
自吾執斧斤以隨夫子未嘗見材如此其美也
先生不肯視行不輟
曰已矣勿言之矣散木也以為舟則沈
以為棺槨則速腐
以為器則速毀
以為門戶則液樠
以為柱則蠹是不材之木也
无所可用故能若是之壽

After Shih the carpenter had returned home, the sacred oak appeared to him in a dream, saying, "What are you comparing me with? Are you comparing me with useful trees? There are cherry, apple, pear, orange, citron, pomelo, and other fruit trees. As soon as the fruit is ripe, the trees are stripped and abused. Their large branches are split, and the smaller ones torn off. Their life is bitter because of their usefulness. That is why they do not live out their natural lives but are cut off in their prime. They attract the attentions of the common world. This is so for all things. As for me, I have been trying for a long time to be useless. I was almost destroyed several times. Finally I am useless, and this is very useful to me. If I had been useful, could I have ever grown so large?

"Besides, you and I are both things. How can one thing judge another thing? What does a dying and worthless man like you know about a worthless tree?" Shih the carpenter awoke and tried to understand his dream.

His apprentice said, "If it had so great a desire to be useless, why does it serve as a shrine?"

Shih the carpenter said, "Hush! Stop talking! It is just pretending to be one so that it will not be hurt by those who do not know it is useless. If it had not become a sacred tree, it would probably have been cut down. It protects itself in a different way from ordinary things. We will miss the point if we judge it in the ordinary way."

Nan Po Tsu Chi was wandering in the Shang Hills when he caught sight of a huge, extraordinary tree. A thousand four-horse chariots could have rested in its shade. Tsu Chi said, "What kind of tree is this? It must be very special wood." He looked up and saw that the smaller branches were gnarled and twisted, and could not be used for beams or rafters. He looked down and saw that the great trunk was curved and knotted, and could not be used for coffins. When he tasted a leaf, it burned his mouth; when he sniffed it, he became intoxicated and for three days acted as if he were drunk. Tsu Chi said, "Indeed, this tree is good for nothing. No wonder it grew so big. That is how it is! Holy men treasure this worthlessness."

Ching Shih in the province of Sung is a good place for growing catalpa, cypress, and mulberry trees. Those trees that attain the girth of a span or more are cut down to make monkey perches. Those of three or four spans are cut down to make beams for tall, elegant houses. Those of seven or eight spans are cut down to make side boards for the coffins of aristocratic and rich merchant families.

So, these trees never achieve their full stature but fall in their prime under the blows of the ax. Such are the hazards of being useful.

In the same way, oxen with white foreheads, pigs with turned-up snouts, and men with piles may not be sacrificed to the River God. Shamans believe these creatures bring bad luck. Holy men, however, believe they are very fortunate.

支離疏者頤隱於臍肩高於頂會撮指天五管在上兩髀為脅
挫鍼治繲足以餬口鼓筴播精足以食十人上徵武士
則支離攘臂而遊於其間上有大役
則支離以有常疾不受功
上與病者粟則受三鍾與十束薪
夫支離其形者
猶足以養其身
終其天年
又況支離其德者乎

There was once a hunchback called Shu. His chin rested on his navel, his shoulders rose up over his head, and his neck bone pointed to the sky. His five vital organs were upside down, and his hips were level with his ribs. By sewing and taking in laundry, he made enough to feed himself. By winnowing and sifting grain, he earned enough to support ten people. When the authorities were raising an army, he came and went without having to hide. When a big public project was planned, he was assigned no work because he was a chronic invalid. When the government was giving free grain to the sick, he received three measures and ten bundles of firewood. If a man whose body is strange can take care of himself and live to the end of his natural life, how much easier it is for a man with strange behavior.

孔子適楚楚狂接輿遊其門曰鳳兮鳳兮

何如德之衰也來世不可待往世不可追也

天下有道聖人成焉天下無道聖人生焉

方今之時僅免刑焉福輕乎羽莫之知載

禍重乎地莫之知避已乎已乎臨人以德

殆乎殆乎畫地而趨迷陽迷陽

无傷吾行吾行郤曲无傷吾足

山木自寇也膏火自煎也

桂可食故伐之漆可用故割之

人皆知有用之用而莫知无用之用也

When Confucius was in the state of Chu, the madman of Chu, Chieh Yu, stood at his gate and cried, "O phoenix, O phoenix, how virtue has declined! One cannot wait for the future. One cannot chase after the past. When Tao is in the world, the sage achieves perfection; when Tao is absent, the sage merely bides his time. In times like these the best you can do is to stay out of trouble. Happiness is as light as a feather, but nobody knows how to bear it. Calamity is as heavy as the earth, but nobody knows how to avoid it. Enough! Enough of this confronting people with virtue! Beware! Beware of trudging down this marked path. Oh, thorns, thorns! You do not block my way. My path twists around you. You do not hurt my feet.

"The mountain trees ask to be chopped down. Fat added to the fire consumes itself. The cinnamon tree is edible, so it is cut down. The lacquer tree is useful, so it is slashed. Everyone knows the usefulness of the useful, but no one knows the usefulness of the useless."

CHAPTER FIVE

SIGNS OF
FULL VIRTUE

In the state of Lu, there was a man named Wang Tai who had but one foot. He had as many followers as Confucius. Chang Chi asked Confucius, "This Wang Tai is a cripple, yet he has as many followers in the state of Lu as you do. When he stands up, he does not teach. When he sits down, he utters no word. People go to him empty, and come back full. Is there such a thing as teaching without words? Can the mind be perfect while the body is deformed? What kind of man is he?"

Confucius said, "This man is a sage. It is just that I have been a little slow in going to see him. I myself am going to make him my teacher. Why shouldn't all of you who are my disciples do the same? I shall bring the whole world, not just the state of Lu, to sit at his feet."

Chang Chi said, "He is a cripple, yet he can be your teacher. He must be quite an extraordinary man. What is unique about the way he uses his mind?"

Confucius said, "Death and life are important, yet they do not affect him. Heaven and earth may collapse, yet he remains unmoved. He perceives the true reality and is not affected by external appearances. He lets things change naturally, and so he holds fast to the roots."

Chang Chi said, "What do you mean?"

Confucius said, "If we observe things from the point of view of their differences, liver and gall are as unlike one another as the state of Chu in the west and the state of Yueh in the east. If we see that which is the same in all things, then the ten thousand things are one. He who sees things in this light is not distracted by what reaches him through his ears and his eyes but lets his mind follow the natural harmony. He sees all things as one and is not troubled by loss. To him, the loss of his foot is just like throwing away so much dirt."

常季自得るも以て知るを志以て志ゆ天青心
物ける身那之都仲他色と人草贈れて流れ
川膳れて北化乙止執日常止学命那れ地や
隹将相独や在冬多青青学命那れ天
唯隣独や止幸神止生以て止収生
夫保収之微羅催之寒角乜人だの手九年
将れ丸之弁自安を収独若牛
雲流堂天地な刀執自寒之骸
家子月一知之好色応圭喜死を申
彼見掃日空掃得人角応集や
彼見何旨以知ゐる子申

Chang Chi said, "He is for himself. He uses his knowledge to perfect his mind and he uses his mind to attain the universal mind. Why do people turn to him in such numbers?"

Confucius said, "Men cannot see their reflection in running water but only in still water. Only that which is still in itself can still the seekers of stillness. Of those things that receive life from the earth, the pine and cypress trees alone stand out. They remain green summer and winter long. Of those that receive life from heaven, the wise King Shun alone was upright. Being fortunate, he was able to order his own life and thus order the lives of others. Holding fast to one's own roots is the foundation of courage. A single brave soldier may overcome nine armies. If he can do this simply because he wants recognition, how much more can be done by one who rules heaven and earth, who embraces the ten thousand things, who dwells only for a time in the body, whose ears and eyes are just for forming images, who unifies all knowledge and never experiences death? He will soon, at a time of his own choosing, leave the dusty world and rise to another level. The world will naturally follow him. Why should he be concerned with the affairs of the world?"

Shen Tu Chia had had his foot cut off as punishment. He and Tsu Chan, the Prime Minister of the state of Cheng, were students of Po Hun Wu Jen.

Tsu Chan said to Shen Tu Chia, "If I leave first, you will stay behind. If you leave first, I will stay behind."

The next day they were once more sitting together in the hall on the same mat. Tsu Chan said to Shen Tu Chia, "If I leave first, you will stay behind. If you leave first, I will stay behind. Now that I am about to leave, will you stay behind or not? I might add that when you see me, you do not even move out of the way. Perhaps you think that you are the equal of a Prime Minister?"

Shen Tu Chia said, "In our master's house is there such a thing as a Prime Minister? Perhaps you are proud of being a Prime Minister and being above everybody. I have heard that if a mirror is bright, dust and dirt will not settle on it. If they do, then it is not really bright. If one remains with a wise man for a long time, one will be without faults. Now, you are seeking great things from our master, yet you still talk like this. Is this proper?"

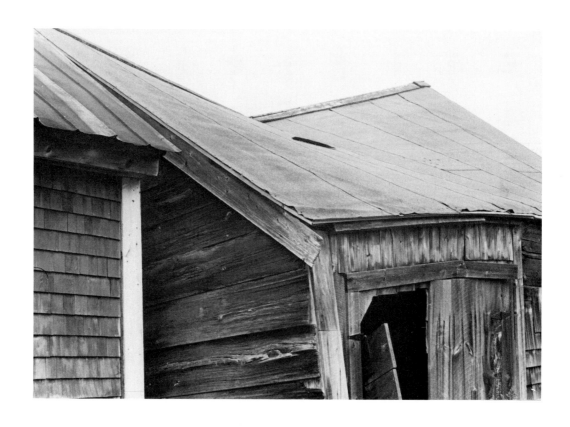

申徒嘉兀者也而與鄭子產同師於伯昏無人
子產謂申徒嘉曰我先出則子止子先出則我止
其明日又與合堂同席而坐子產謂申徒嘉曰
我先出則子止子先出則我止今我將出子可以止乎
其未邪且子見執政而不違子齊執政乎
申徒嘉曰先生之門固有執政焉如此哉
子而說子之執政而後人者也
聞之曰鑑明則塵垢不止止則不明也
久與賢人處則無過今子之所取大者先生也
而猶出言若是不亦過乎

Tsu Chan said, "Take a look at yourself! You still think that you can be as good as Yao. Examine your virtues. Perhaps you will have cause to reflect."

Shen Tu Chia said, "Those who justify their faults to avoid punishment are many, and those who do not justify their faults and refuse to be spared are few. But only the virtuous man can resign himself to the inevitable and accept it as fate. Those who wander in front of archer Yi's target will be hit. If they do not get hit, it is fate. Many people who have both feet laugh at me for having only one. I used to explode with anger. Since I came to study with the Master, I have changed completely. Perhaps he has washed me clean with his goodness. I have been with the Master for nineteen years, and I have never been aware of having only one foot. Now, you and I are supposed to be concerned with our inner selves and yet you pay attention to my external body. Is this proper?"

Tsu Chan was disconcerted, his expression changed, and he asked Shen Tu Chia to say no more.

子産曰子晳若是美犹自克甚其重喜計其言也自邑
申信嘉邑自邑矣過而不言由言有其害也
死乃而奉有寄安之若命塗有寇矣然之也逝邗水野之野中
申余野中也之及不也乎命也爲失重爲之笑而之之吾吾不爲多矣
牛博盆亦怒盡邑先生之及勿勝彼爲而乎先生之免邑而喜邑
言邑吾吾之好大牛也事之歌盡爲之邑免邑而喜邑
子産疏然爲邑寄之題日子元乃
孫

There was a cripple in Lu named Shu Shan No-toes. He came walking on his heels to see Confucius. Confucius said, "You did not take care. You committed a crime and brought this trouble upon yourself. What is the use of coming to me now?"

No-toes said, "I didn't know how to behave properly, and took my body lightly, so I lost my toes. I have come here with something more precious than toes, and it is this which I seek to preserve. There is nothing that heaven does not cover. There is nothing that earth does not sustain. I thought that you, Master, were like heaven and earth. How was I to know that you would receive me this way?"

Confucius said, "It was stupid of me. Why don't you come in! Let us talk."

But No-toes walked out.

Confucius said, "This is a good lesson, disciples! A toeless cripple is still willing to atone for his past misdeeds. How much more can be done by those who haven't had such bad luck."

No-toes went to see Lao Tsu and said, "Is Confucius not yet a perfect man? Why does he keep imitating you? He is trying to gain a reputation by pretending to know strange and extraordinary things. He does not know that real sages look upon these as cuffs and fetters."

Lao Tsu said, "Why don't you simply make him see that life and death are one thread, the same line viewed from different sides—and thus free him from his cuffs and fetters? Is that possible?"

No-toes said, "If heaven wants to punish him, who can free him?"

Duke Ai of Lu asked Confucius, "In Wei, there was an ugly man by the name of Ai Tai To. Yet the men around him thought so much of him, they could never leave him. When young ladies saw him, they told their parents that they would rather be his concubines than other men's wives. There were ten or more such cases. He never tried to lead others but always went along with people. He was never in the position of a ruler who could protect people's lives. He was not a wealthy man who could fill people's bellies. Moreover, he was hideous enough to scare everything under heaven. He agreed with people but never persuaded them. He knew only what happened in the place where he lived. Yet both men and women sought his company. There must have been something extraordinary about him, I thought. So I summoned him for an interview, and indeed he was frighteningly ugly. Yet within the first month that he was with me, I began to see that there was something in that man, and within a year I completely trusted him. As my state needed a Prime Minister, I offered him the position. He was reluctant to give a reply, and was evasive as though he wanted to refuse. That made me feel ashamed, and finally I handed over the government to him. Soon after that, he went away and left me. I was so sad, it was as if I were in mourning. I no longer had anyone with whom I could share the joy of my state. What kind of man was that?"

Confucius said, "Once when I was on a mission to the state of Chu, I saw some little pigs sucking their dead mother. After a while, they suddenly looked at her. Then they all ran away and left her because she did not look back at them. She was no longer like themselves. What they loved in their mother was not her body but that which made her body alive. When a man is killed in battle and is buried, he has no use for medals. When a man has no feet, he does not care about shoes. Both men have lost something essential. The King's concubines do not trim their nails or pierce their ears. When a man is newly married, he stays away from his official duties and is not sent on missions. Such is the importance of keeping the body whole. How much more important to preserve virtue. Now, Ai Tai To said nothing and was trusted. He achieved nothing and was loved. So someone offered him the government, and was only afraid that he would refuse. He must have achieved full harmony without any outward manifestation of virtue."

Duke Ai asked, "What do you mean by achieving full harmony?"

Confucius said, "Life and death, profit and loss, failure and success, poverty and wealth, value and worthlessness, praise and blame, hunger and thirst, cold and heat—these are natural changes in the order of things. They alternate with one another like day and night. No one knows where one ends and the other begins. Therefore, they should not disturb our peace or enter into our souls. Live so that you are at ease, in harmony with the world, and full of joy. Day and night, share the springtime with all things, thus creating the seasons in your own heart. This is called achieving full harmony."

"And what is this lack of outward manifestation of virtue?"

Confucius said, "Balance is the perfect state of still water. Let that be our model. It remains quiet within and is not disturbed on the surface. Virtue is the attainment of perfect harmony. Because

virtue has no outward form, nothing can escape from it."

Later, Duke Ai told this to Ming Tsu, saying, "When I first faced south and took the reins of government, guiding the people and caring for their lives, I thought that I was doing my utmost as a ruler. Now that I have heard the words of a perfect man, I am afraid that there is no substance to what I am doing. I have foolishly squandered my energy and am ruining my country. Confucius and I are no longer related as subject and ruler but as spiritual companions."

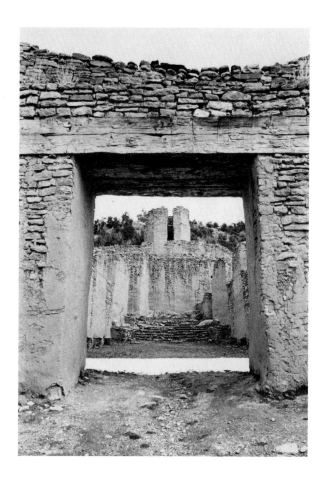

Clubfoot-Hunchback-No-lips talked to Duke Ling of Wei. Duke Ling was so delighted with him that when he saw normal people, their necks appeared thin and scraggy. Jug-Jar-Big-goiter talked to Duke Huan of Chi. Duke Huan was so delighted with him that when he saw normal people, he too thought their necks were thin and scraggy. So when goodness shines forth, the outward appearances are forgotten. Men do not forget what ought to be forgotten, but forget what ought not be forgotten. This is forgetfulness indeed! Therefore, the sage lets everything pass before his mind. To him learning is something added, conventions are like glue, morality is a bond, and skills are for trade. The sage does not make plans, so what use has he for learning? He does not make divisions, so what use has he for glue? He lacks nothing, so what use has he for morality? He has nothing to sell, so what use has he for trade? His not needing these four things is a gift from heaven. This gift is his heavenly food. Since he is fed by heaven, what use has he for men? He has the appearance of a man but not the desires of a man. He has the appearance of a man, so he associates with men. He does not have the desires of a man, so he is not concerned with right or wrong. How infinitely small is that which makes him a man! How infinitely great is that which makes him perfect in heaven!

Hui Tsu asked Chuang Tsu, "Can a man really live without desire?"

"Yes," said Chuang Tsu.

"But," said Hui Tsu, "if a man has no desire, how can you call him a man?"

Chuang Tsu said, "Tao gives him his appearance, and heaven gives him his body. Why should he not be called a man?"

Hui Tsu said, "Since he is called a man, how can he be without desire?"

Chuang Tsu said, "That is not what I mean by desire. When I say he has no desire I mean that he does not disturb his inner well-being with likes and dislikes. He accepts things as they are and does not try to improve upon them."

Hui Tsu said, "If a man does not try to improve upon the way things are, how does he survive?"

Chuang Tsu said, "Tao gives him his appearance. Heaven gives him his body. He does not disturb his inner well-being with likes and dislikes. At present you use all your vital energy on external things and wear out your spirit. You lean against a tree and mutter, collapse upon a rotten stump and fall asleep. Your body is a gift from heaven, yet you use it to babble and jabber about 'hardness' and 'whiteness'!"

惠子曰莊子曰人固不知魚之樂
莊子曰子非我安知我不知魚之樂
莊子與惠子遊於濠梁之上莊子曰
鯈魚出遊從容是魚之樂也惠子曰
子非魚安知魚之樂莊子曰子非我
安知我不知魚之樂惠子曰我非子
固不知子矣子固非魚也子之不知
魚之樂全矣莊子曰請循其本子曰
汝安知魚樂云者既已知吾知之而
問我我知之濠上也

CHAPTER SIX

THE GREAT
MASTER

知天之所為而知人之所為者至矣天之所為

以天之所為を以□り天之所為不を

終天年而不中道夭者を之盛や□□

有患夫を有所待而□當や□□

雖然を□所語天之乱人ま所語人之乱天ま

且有□人而□有□也

Perfect is the man who knows what comes
from heaven and what comes from man.
Knowing what comes from heaven, he is
in tune with heaven. Knowing what
comes from man, he uses his knowledge
of the known to develop his knowledge
of the unknown and enjoys the fullness of
life until his natural death. This is the
perfection of knowledge. However, there
is one difficulty. Knowledge must be
based upon something, but one is not
certain what this may be. How, indeed,
do I know that what I call heaven is not
actually man, and that what I call man is
not actually heaven? First, there must be
a true man; then there can be true
knowledge.

But what is a true man? The true man of old did not mind being poor. He took no pride in his achievements. He made no plans. Thus, he could commit an error and not regret it. He could succeed without being proud. Thus, he could climb mountains without fear, enter water without getting wet, and pass through fire unscathed. This is the knowledge that leads to Tao.

The true man of old slept without dreaming and woke without anxiety. His food was plain, and his breath was deep. For the breath of the true man rose up from his heels while the breath of common men rises from their throats. When they are overcome, their words catch in their throats like vomit. As their lusts and desires deepen, their heavenly nature grows shallow.

The true man of old knew nothing about loving life or hating death. When he was born, he felt no elation. When he entered death, there was no sorrow. Carefree he went. Carefree he came. That was all. He did not forget his beginning and did not seek his end. He accepted what he was given with delight, and when it was gone, he gave it no more thought. This is called not using the mind against Tao and not using man to help heaven. Such was the true man.

若松や志ら志天堂最天気顥憂苑似狹燵苑似春
嘉思週の時お畑百貫而有天を天極
坂船里人三田気や上爾而下志忘刹里獅子万両
ひ子爰へ坂出週狗苑雪久や有欲苑仁や
大財苑似賢や利宝石週紀子天や刹和生を
苑士やミ引え無苑紀人や若狐ミ候稀を
伯母叔稀算其子骨飯仁や申待狀
是役人ミ役言週人ミ南而不月南週天南た乃

Such a man has a free mind, a calm manner, and an unfurrowed brow. He is as cool as autumn and as mild as spring. His joy and anger flow like changing seasons. He is in harmony with all things and has no limitations. Therefore, when a wise man wages war, he can destroy a nation without losing the people's hearts. His blessings fall upon the ten thousand things, but not because he loves men.

Therefore, the man who desires to know all things is not a sage. Showing partiality is not true kindness. He who calculates his timing is not a man of wisdom. He who does not see through gain and loss is not a great man. He who seeks recognition and does not follow what he knows is not a man of understanding. He who would lose his life without being true to himself can never be a master of men. Such men as Hu Pu Chieh, Wu Kuang, Po I, Shu Chi, Chi Tsu, Hsu Yu, Chi To, and Shen Tu Ti all lost their lives by doing the bidding of others. They tried to act in ways that were natural to others but not natural to themselves.

This was the true man of old. He stood straight and firm and did not waver. He was of humble mien but was not servile. He was independent but not stubborn, open to everything yet made no boast. He smiled as if pleased, and responded to things naturally. His radiance came from his inner light. He remained centered even in the company of others. He was broadminded as if he agreed with everyone, high-minded as if beyond influence, inward-minded as if he would like to withdraw from the world, and absentminded as if unaware of what he was going to say. He considered criminal law to be the body of government, ceremony its wings, knowledge a requirement of the times, and reason a guide for action. To consider law as the body, one has to be lenient in its execution. To take ceremony as the wings is to give people something to follow. To take knowledge as a requirement of the times is to do things that have to be done. To consider reason as a guide for action is to be with others on the path upward. He acted effortlessly, yet people thought that he was trying very hard.

What he likes is the One; what he does not like is also the One. That which is One is One; that which is not One is also One. He knows the One and is of heaven. He knows not the One and is of men. So heaven and men are not in conflict. Such is the true man. It is destiny to live and die, as certain as night and day. It is of heaven, beyond the interference of men.

Such is the nature of things. If a man is willing to view heaven as his father and experiences love, how much more love will he feel for what is beyond heaven! If he feels that the ruler of the kingdom is above him and he is willing to die for the king, how much more will he be willing to do for the truth!

When the springs go dry and fish are left stranded on the ground, they smear each other with slime and spew spit on one another. It is better for them to be in the rivers and lakes, where they pay each other no heed. Instead of praising Yao and denouncing Chieh, it would be better to pay heed to neither and lose oneself in Tao.

敬天ゆゑや一天帝ぬるや一天一や一
天ろ一や一天一与夫而後
天ろ一与、而後天与人不相勝や
ゆゑ之説や旨一真人
死生命や天有権日二之常而天也
今之有所不由島此物之情や
彼特以天而父可旬犹愛之
而况天卓乎
人特以有見而愈まつ而旬犹死天真ず
泉涸魚相与处于陸相喣以湿相濡以沫不如
相忘乎江湖与其誉尭而死桀

121

夫大塊載我以形、勞我以生、佚我以老、息我以死、故善吾生者、乃所以善吾死也。夫藏舟於壑、藏山於澤、謂之固矣。然而夜半有力者負之而走、昧者不知也。藏小大有宜、猶有所遯。若夫藏天下於天下而不得所遯、是恒物之大情也。特犯人之形而猶喜之、若人之形者、萬化而未始有極也、其為樂可勝計邪。故聖人將遊於物之所不得遯而皆存。善妖善老、善始善終、人猶效之、又況萬物之所係而一化之所待乎。

The great earth burdens me with a body, causes me to toil in life, eases me in old age, and rests me in death. That which makes my life good, makes my death good also.

A boat concealed in a ravine and a fish net in a swamp appear to be safely hidden. But at midnight a strong man may put them on his back and walk off with them. Dimwits do not understand that no matter how well one hides small things in larger ones, there is always a chance of losing them. But if you hide the universe in the universe, there is no way to lose it. This is the ultimate reality.

You were born in a human form, and you find joy in it. Yet there are ten thousand other forms endlessly transforming that are equally good, and the joy in these is untold. The sage dwells among those things which can never be lost, and so he lives forever. He willingly accepts early death, old age, the beginning and the end, and serves as an example for everyone. How much more should we emulate the creator of the ten thousand things, on whom the great flow depends!

夫ゟ有たゝ有信元も元形も偽もてゝ営もね而ふも見
自本自根未有天地月ちゝ圉な神鬼神常も天もや
左右极之先而ふも高宜之ゝ梠之下而ふも窂
先天地光而ふめ久たろ于正古而ふめ老猶蒙中氏ろ
以扨手天坤伏戯氏ゆて以雀花氣ゝ於斗ゆる之於古不戌
日月ゐ之翁ち不自埕坯ゆて以雀死囲乢崎崘馬夷ゐゝ遊太川
育めろ便てゝ処士山頂ゝ帝囲之以陸そ天郷北囲之以処言宮
愚诤由ゝ之守北极一而豆囲て坐さ方廣草先老ゟ
莫色之郷彰疤ゆ之上廖 有寓下及ろ伯
傳说狸之以狸ぜ丁奄 有天下乘东ゝ驕笑尾而狂于刿日畢

124

Tao has reality and substance, but no action or form. It can be given but not received. It is attainable but invisible. It is its own source and its own root. It existed before heaven and earth and for all eternity. It causes spirits and gods to be divine. It begets heaven and earth. It is above the zenith and yet not high. It is below the nadir and yet not low. It was born before heaven and earth but not long ago. It was there before the oldest antiquity but is not old.

Hsi Wei attained Tao and brought heaven and earth into harmony. Fu Hsi attained it and entered into the source of vital energy. The Great Bear attained it and has never erred from its course. The sun and moon attained it and have never ceased to shine. Kan Pi attained it and entered Kunlun Mountain. Feng I attained it and wandered along the Great River. Chien Wu attained it and dwelt on Mount Tai. The Yellow Emperor attained it and soared upon the clouds to heaven. Chuan Hsu attained it and dwelt in the Dark Palace. Yu Chiang attained it and went to live at the North Pole. The Queen Mother of the West attained it and took her seat on Shao Kwan Mountain. No one knows her beginning and no one knows her end. Peng Tsu attained it and lived from the time of Shun to the time of the Five Princes. Fu Yueh attained it, became Prime Minister to Wu Ting, and ruled the world. Then he mounted the eastern Milky Way, and riding on Sagittarius and Scorpio, he took his place among the constellations.

Nan Po Tsu Kuei asked Hunchback Woman, "You are old, and yet you look like a child. Why is this?"

"I have found Tao," she replied.

"Can Tao be learned?" he asked.

"No! How could it be? You are not the one to do it, anyway. Now, consider Pu Liang I. He has the talent of a sage but not the Tao of a sage. I have the Tao of a sage but not the talent. I wished to teach him so that he might indeed be a sage. Teaching the Tao of a sage to one who has the talent of a sage seems to be an easy matter. But no, it took a long time to reveal it to him. After three days, he began to transcend the physical world. After his transcendence of the physical world, I kept working with him. After seven days, he began to transcend all material existence. After his transcendence of all material existence, I kept working with him. After nine days, he began to transcend all life. Having transcended all life, he began to achieve the clear vision of dawn. Having achieved the clear vision of dawn, he began to see the One. Having seen the One, he began to transcend the distinction of past and present. Having transcended the distinction of past and present, he began to enter the land where there is no life or death, where killing does not take away life and giving birth does not add to it. He would reject nothing, welcomed all things, negated all things, and affirmed all things. This is called tranquillity in struggle, meaning perfection is the result of struggle."

Nan Po Tsu Kuei asked, "Where did you learn all this?"

She replied, "I have learned it from the son of Ink-writing, the son of Ink-writing from the grandson of Chanting-recitation, the grandson of Chanting-recitation from Clear-understanding, Clear-understanding from Quiet-affirmation, Quiet-affirmation from Immediate-experience, Immediate-experience from Dramatic-expression, Dramatic-expression from Dark-obscurity, Dark-obscurity from Mysterious-void, and Mysterious-void from Beginning-of-no-beginning."

Four men, Tsu Szu, Tsu Yu, Tsu Li, and Tsu Lai, were having a discussion, saying, "Whoever believes Nothingness to be the head, Life to be the backbone, and Death to be the tail; whoever can know life, death, being, and non-being all as one, shall be our friend." The four looked at one another and smiled. And since they were in complete agreement, they became fast friends.

Not long after, Tsu Yu fell ill, and Tsu Szu went to see him. Tsu Yu said, "Great is the Maker of Things that He should make me as deformed as this!"

His crooked spine was curled round like a hunchback; his five organs were upside down; his chin rested on his navel; his shoulders rose up above his head; his neckbone pointed to the sky. His body was sick, yet he was calm and carefree. He limped to the well and looked at his reflection and said, "Ah! The Maker of Things has made me all crooked like this!"

"Does this upset you?" asked Tsu Szu.

"No, why should it? If my left arm became a rooster, I would use it to herald the dawn. If my right arm became a crossbow, I would shoot down a bird for roasting. If my buttocks became wheels and my spirits a horse, I would ride them. What need would I have for a wagon? For we were born because it was time, and we die in accordance with nature. If we are content with whatever happens and follow the flow, joy and sorrow cannot affect us. This is what the ancients called freedom from bondage. There are those who cannot free themselves because they are bound by material existence. But nothing can overcome heaven. That is the way it has always been. Why should I be upset?"

莊子妻死，惠子弔之，莊子則方箕踞鼓盆而歌。惠子曰：「與人居，長子老身死，不哭亦足矣，又鼓盆而歌，不亦甚乎！」莊子曰：「不然。是其始死也，我獨何能無概然！察其始而本無生，非徒無生也而本無形，非徒無形也而本無氣。雜乎芒芴之間，變而有氣，氣變而有形，形變而有生，今又變而之死，是相與為春秋冬夏四時行也。人且偃然寢於巨室，而我噭噭然隨而哭之，自以為不通乎命，故止也。」

Shortly, thereafter, Tsu Lai fell ill. He lay gasping for life while his wife and children gathered around crying. Tsu Li came to see him and said, "Shhh! Get away from him! Do not disturb the transformation!" Leaning against the door, he said to Tsu Lai, "Great is the Maker! What will He use you for now? Where will He send you? Will He make you into a rat's gizzard or a snake's leg?"

Tsu Lai replied, "A son must go wherever his parents tell him to go! East, west, south, or north. Yin and Yang are no other than one's parents. If they brought me to the verge of death and I do not obey them, then I am only being stubborn. They are not to be blamed.

The great earth burdens me with a body, causes me to toil in life, eases me in old age, and rests me in death. That which makes my life good makes my death good also. If a skilled smith were casting metal and the metal should leap up and say, 'Make me into a famous sword like Mo Yeh!' the smith would surely consider it an ill omen. Now, if by chance I were being cast into a human form and I were to say, 'Make me a man! Make me a man!' the Maker of Things would certainly consider me an ill omen. Now, if I regard heaven and earth as a great melting pot and creation and transformation as a master smith, then where can I be sent and not find it fitting? Thus, calmly I sleep and freshly I waken."

Tsu Sang Hu, Meng Tsu Fan, and Tsu Chin Chang were acquaintances. They said to each other, "Who can be together without togetherness and cooperate without cooperation? Who can soar up to heaven, wander through the clouds, and pass beyond the limits of space, unmindful of existence, forever and ever?" Then the three looked at one another and laughed. Having no disagreement among themselves, they became fast friends.

After some time, Tsu Sang Hu died. Before the burial, Confucius heard of his death and sent his disciple Tsu Kung to attend the mourning. Tsu Kung found that one of the friends was composing a song and the other was playing a lute.

They sang together in unison, "Oh Sang Hu! Oh Sang Hu! You have gone back to your true self while we remain as men. Alas! Alas!"

Tsu Kung hurried in and said, "May I ask something? Is that appropriate, singing in the presence of a corpse?"

The two looked at each other and laughed. "What does he know about ceremony?" they said.

子貢反、以告孔子、曰、彼何人者邪、修行無有、而外其形骸、臨尸而歌、顏色不變、無以命之、
彼何人者邪、孔子曰、彼遊方之外者也、而丘遊方之內者也、外內不相及、
而丘使女往弔之、丘則陋矣、彼方且與造物者為人、而遊乎天地之一氣、
彼以生為附贅縣疣、以死為決𤺏潰癰、夫若然者、又惡知死生先後之所在、
假於異物、託於同體、忘其肝膽、遺其耳目、反覆終始、不知端倪、
芒然彷徨乎塵垢之外、逍遙乎無為之業、彼又惡能憒憒然為世俗之禮、
以觀眾人之耳目哉、子貢曰、然則夫子何方之依、
孔子曰、丘、天之戮民也、雖然、吾與汝共之、
子貢曰、敢問其方、孔子曰、魚相造乎水、人相造乎道、
相造乎水者、穿池而養給、相造乎道者、無事而生定、
故曰、魚相忘乎江湖、人相忘乎道術、
子貢曰、敢問畸人、曰、畸人者、畸於人而侔於天、
故曰、天之小人、人之君子、人之君子、天之小人也、

Tsu Kung went back and reported to Confucius, saying, "What sort of men are they? They are badly behaved and are unconcerned with appearances. They sang in front of the corpse with no sign of emotion. I do not know how to describe them. What sort of people are they?"

Confucius said, "They travel beyond the physical world, and I travel within it. Our paths will never meet. It was stupid of me to send you to attend the funeral. They are now in the company of the Maker of Things and are taking delight in the one breath of heaven and earth. They look upon life as a swelling tumor, a protruding goiter, and look upon death as the bursting of a boil and the draining of an abscess. How could such men discriminate between life and death? They consider the body as an accidental arrangement of different elements. They forget their livers and galls, and ignore their eyes and ears. They come and go, ending and beginning again, unmindful of any limitations. Without a care, they roam beyond the dusty world and wander freely, dwelling in non-action. Why should they bother with the conventions of this vulgar world and make a show for the eyes and ears of the common people?"

Tsu Kung said, "Why then, Master, do you observe conventions?"

Confucius said, "I am condemned by heaven to do so. However, you and I have this in common."

Tsu Kung said, "May I ask what you mean?"

Confucius said, "Fish thrive in water; men thrive in Tao. Those who thrive in water dart about in the pond and find nourishment there. Those who thrive in Tao work without doing, and their nature is realized. Therefore, it is said, 'Fish need to lose themselves in rivers and lakes, and men need to lose themselves in the practice of Tao.'"

Tsu Kung said, "May I ask about those strange people?"

"The strange people are strange to men but familiar to heaven. Therefore, it is said, 'The inferior man of heaven is superior among men; the inferior man among men is superior in heaven.'"

Yen Hui asked Confucius, "When Meng Sun Tsai's mother died, he cried out but did not weep. He was not sad at heart. He observed mourning without sorrow. With these three failings, he was nevertheless considered the best mourner in the state of Lu. How can one gain such a reputation on nothing? I am utterly amazed!"

Confucius said, "Meng Sun has indeed mastered Tao! He has gone beyond wisdom. He has already made his life simple. Yet there are certain customs he still has to observe. Meng Sun does not know why we live and why we die. He does not know which comes first and which last. He accepts his state of being without concern for future transformation. When one is changing, how does one know that a change is taking place? When one is not changing, how does one know that a change hasn't already occurred? Maybe you and I are still in a dream and have not yet awakened. Moreover, Meng Sun appeared shaken, but his mind was not moved. There was a change of abode, but there was no real death. Meng Sun was the only one who was awake. He wept only when he saw the others weep; that is his true nature. Furthermore, we all talk about 'me.' How do we know that there is such a person as 'me'? You dream that you are a bird soaring up to the sky. You dream that you are a fish diving in a pool. As we speak now, we do not know whether we are awake or dreaming. Making accusations is not as good as laughing. And laughter is not as good as letting things follow their natural course. Be content with what is happening and forget about change; then you can enter into the oneness of the mystery of heaven."

Yi Erh Tsu went to see Hsu Yu. Hsu Yu asked, "What has Yao taught you?"

Yi Erh Tsu said, "Yao instructed me to practice kindness and goodness and to distinguish clearly between right and wrong."

Hsu Yu said, "Then why do you come to see me? Yao has already branded you with kindness and goodness and cut off your nose with right and wrong. How will you be able to wander on the path, freely and without a care, doing whatever you like?"

Yi Erh Tsu said, "That may be so, but I would still like to wander along the fringes if I can."

Hsu Yu said, "No, when a man is blind, it is impossible for him to appreciate the beauty of face and complexion or to tell a blue sacrificial robe from a yellow one."

Yi Erh Tsu said, "Wu Chuang surrendered her beauty, Chu Liang abandoned his strength, and the Yellow Emperor discarded his knowledge. All of these were part of a process of purging and purification. How do you know that the Maker of Things would not rid me of my brands, replace my nose, and make me fit to be your disciple?"

Hsu Yu said, "Ah! We cannot tell yet. But let me give you the general idea. O my master! O my master! he set the ten thousand things in order, yet he does not consider himself good. He gave life to the ten thousand generations, yet he does not consider himself kind. He is more ancient than the oldest antiquity, yet he does not consider himself old. He covers heaven, sustains the earth, carves and fashions all forms, yet he does not consider himself skillful. I follow him."

Yen Hui said, "I am making progress."

Confucius asked, "In what way?"

Yen Hui said, "I have given up doing good and being right."

Confucius said, "Very good, but that is not quite enough."

Another day, Yen Hui saw Confucius and said, "I am making progress."

Confucius asked, "In what way?"

Yen Hui said, "I have given up ceremony and music."

Confucius said, "Very good, but that is not quite enough."

Another day, Yen Hui saw Confucius again and said, "I am making progress."

Confucius asked, "In what way?"

Yen Hui said, "I just sit and forget."

Confucius was startled and asked, "What do you mean by sitting and forgetting?"

Yen Hui said, "I am not attached to the body and I give up any idea of knowing. By freeing myself from the body and mind, I become one with the infinite. This is what I mean by sitting and forgetting."

Confucius said, "When there is oneness, there are no preferences. When there is change, there is no constancy. If you have really attained this, then let me become your pupil."

子輿與子桑友，而霖雨十日，子輿曰：子桑殆病矣！裹飯而往食之。至子桑之門，則若歌若哭，鼓琴曰：父邪！母邪！天乎！人乎！有不任其聲而趨舉其詩焉。子輿入，曰：子之歌詩，何故若是？曰：吾思夫使我至此極者而弗得也。父母豈欲吾貧哉？天無私覆，地無私載，天地豈私貧我哉？求其為之者而不得也。然而至此極者，命也夫！

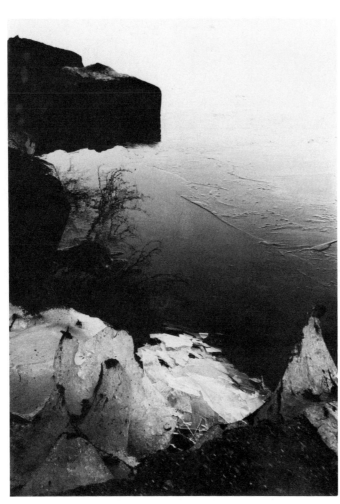

Tsu Yu and Tsu Sang were friends. Once when it had rained for ten days, Tsu Yu said, "Tsu Sang may be having a hard time." So he packed up some food and took it to him. Arriving at Tsu Sang's door, he heard something that was like singing or weeping, accompanied by a lute. "O Father! O Mother! Is it heaven? Or is it man?" The voice was breaking, and the words faltered.

Tsu Yu entered and said, "Why are you chanting poetry like this?"

Tsu Sang said, "I am trying to find out why I am in such a wretched state. I cannot understand it. Would my father and mother have wanted me to be so poor? Heaven provides shelter for things. Earth sustains all things. Would heaven and earth single me out to be poor? I am trying to find the cause of this but cannot see what it is. Yet here I am in my wretchedness. It must be fate."

応帝王

CHAPTER SEVEN

THE SAGE KING

起画欧同于西便四同而四不尽
起画起田踟衄市大喜
行以苦蒲衣子
蒲花子子由而乃以色之
有雲氏不及奉氏
有雲氏决狄藏仁以安人
加得以失宕以收出于纪人
奉氏失卧徐徐
失見于于
一阿て而马
一行そ而生
失を惰信
七庵左屋六柒恼下于纪人

Yeh Chueh was questioning Wang Yi. Four times he asked a question and four times he received no answer. This delighted Yeh Chueh so much, he went to tell Pu Yi Tsu.

Pu Yi Tsu said, "Are you only just finding that out? Emperor Shun was no match for Emperor Fu Shi. Emperor Shun always tried to do good so that men would follow him. He was never able to distinguish between what a man is and what he is not. On the other hand, Emperor Fu Shi was calm and tranquil when asleep, and simple and direct when awake. Sometimes he would take on the spirit of a horse, and sometimes that of an ox. His wisdom could be trusted. His virtue was genuine. He was beyond distinguishing between what a man is and what he is not."

眉毛可見猶猶猶猶與與日日中將何以諭女

有雲自生出更人生以已去強式必發

人執敢不听而似許

犯拯與二日月之故性也

女子將天下也猶仿佛以的聲金日而佐病魚出也

夫聖人之至也而仿如此

正而後行

准于知其夫中之本令如夫

且鳥之為形而以延譽也之官

麗鼠保穴求神立之下

以熏蟄金之患

守軍而更之先也

Chien Wu went to see the madman, Chieh Yu. Chieh Yu said, "What did Chung Shih tell you the other day?"

Chien Wu said, "He told me that a ruler should be an example to others, establishing law and order, ceremony, and measure, so that every man is influenced and is never tempted to break the law."

Chieh Yu said, "This is subverting virtue! Trying to govern the world that way is like wading through the sea, digging a river, or making a mosquito carry a mountain on its back. When a wise man rules, is he concerned with outward appearances? When the mind is clear, then appropriate action follows. Let each man do what he can, that is all. Birds fly high in the sky so as to avoid being hit by stringed arrows. Mice make their homes deep under the sacred mound so as to avoid being smoked out or dug up. Surely men have more sense than these two creatures?"

Tien Ken was traveling on the south side of Mount Yin. When he reached the Liao River, he met a nameless sage to whom he said, "Please tell me how to rule the world."

The nameless sage said, "Go away, you fool! Why do you ask such an improper question? I am about to join the Maker of Things. For enjoyment I ride on the bird of ease and emptiness, out beyond the six directions, wandering in the land of nowhere and dwelling in the domain of nothingness. Why do you bother me with the problem of ruling the world?"

But Tien Ken repeated his question once more. The nameless sage said, "Let your mind wander in the pure and simple. Be one with the infinite. Allow all things to take their course. Do not try to be clever. Then the world will be ruled!"

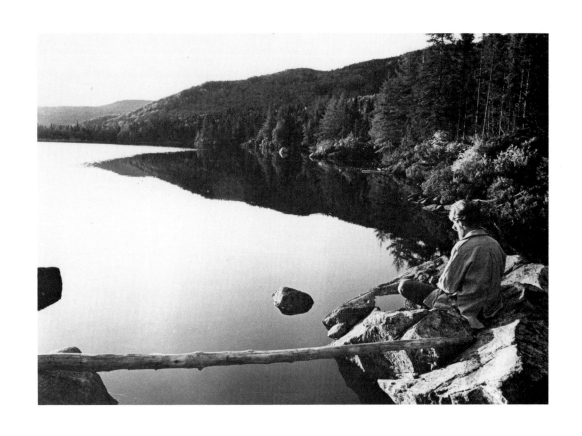

天根遊于殷陽至蓼水之上
適遭無名人而問焉曰請問為天下
天根又問無名人曰汝鄙人也
何問之不豫也予方將與造物者
為人厭則又乘夫莽眇之鳥
以出六極之外而遊無何有之鄉
以處壙埌之野汝又何帛
以治天下感予之心為
汝游心於淡合氣於漠
順物自然而無容私焉
而天下治矣

151

Yang Tsu Chu went to see Lao Tsu and said, "Here is a man who is sensitive, alert, strong, and decisive, with a thorough knowledge of the workings of things and untiring in his study of Tao. Could he be compared with a sage king?"

Lao Tsu said, "In comparison with the sages, such a man is like a hard-working servant, a craftsman intent upon his work, wearing out his body and confusing his mind. It is said that the reason men hunt the tiger and the leopard is the beauty of their skins. The agility of the monkey and the dog's ability to catch rats cause men to domesticate them. So how can such a man be compared with a sage king?"

Yang Tsu Chu was amazed and said, "May I ask how a sage king rules?"

Lao Tsu said, "When a sage king rules, his influence is felt everywhere but he does not seem to be doing anything. His work affects the ten thousand things, but the people do not depend upon him. No one is aware of him, but he brings happiness to every man. He stands on that which is not known and wanders in the land of nowhere."

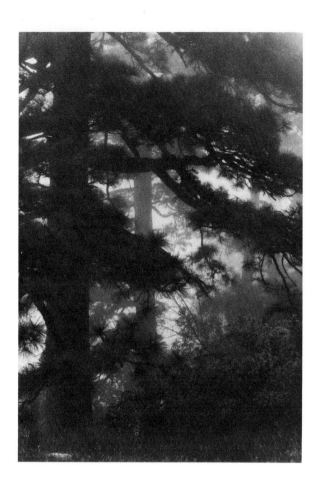

In the state of Cheng, there was a shaman named Chi Hsien. He could tell everything about birth and death, gain and loss, misfortune and happiness, and the length of a man's life, predicting the exact year, month, week, and day as though he were a god. The people of Cheng used to flee at the mere sight of him. Lieh Tsu went to see him and was fascinated. On his return, he said to Hu Tsu, "Master! I used to think that your Tao was perfect. But now I know something more perfect still."

Hu Tsu said, "I have taught you only the letter and not the spirit of Tao. Do you really think that you have mastered Tao? If there is no rooster in a flock of hens, how can they lay fertile eggs? You try to flaunt your knowledge of Tao to make people believe in it.

That is why people can see right through you. Bring the shaman here and I will confront him."

The next day Lieh Tsu brought him to see Hu Tsu. As the shaman left, he remarked, "Alas! Your master is dying. He will not live another ten days. I saw something strange in him. He had the appearance of wet ashes."

His gown drenched with tears, Lieh Tsu went in and told Hu Tsu what he had heard. Hu Tsu said, "Just now I showed him the still and silent earth, the tranquil and motionless mountain. Probably he saw only that I have dammed up the springs of my vital energy. Bring him back again."

The next day the two came again to see Hu Tsu. As the shaman left, he said, "It is fortunate that your master met me. He is getting better already. He is perfectly alive. I can see that the closing up of his energy flow is only temporary."

Lieh Tsu went in and told Hu Tsu. Hu Tsu said, "Just now I showed him the heavenly void without name or substance. My vital energy comes up from my heels. Probably all he saw was my releasing the springs of this energy. Try to bring him back again."

The next day the two went again to see Hu Tsu. As the shaman left, he said, "Your master is never the same. I have no way to read his face. Wait until he settles down, then I shall examine him again."

Lieh Tsu went in and told Hu Tsu. Hu Tsu said, "I have just shown him the ultimate harmony, where there is perfect balance. Probably all he saw was the depths of my vital energy in its perfection. When the waves swirl in a torrent, there are dark depths. When the water is still, there are dark depths. When the water flows, there are also dark depths. There are nine names for the dark depths. I demonstrated only three of them. Try to bring him again."

The next day the two came to see Hu Tsu again. Before they even sat down, the shaman lost his nerve and fled. "Run after him!" Hu Tsu said. Lieh Tsu ran but could not catch up with the shaman, so he returned and said to Hu Tsu, "He has disappeared. He is gone. I could not find him."

Hu Tsu said, "I just showed him what existed before the beginning of things. Completely open and yielding, I showed myself, without a care, like grass bending before the wind and water flowing in waves. That is why he ran away."

Whereupon Lieh Tsu realized that he had not yet begun to understand. He went home, and for the next three years he did not go out. He did the cooking for his wife and fed the pigs as though they were human. He took no interest in worldly affairs. He stopped making complications and returned to simplicity. Rooted in the earth and centered in his body, amid all the confusion and distractions of life, he remained one with Tao until the end of his days.

矢の名は失るゝ謀なを矢るゝ便矢のゑを了能くも矢前
（矢）の脱片も云術學まて天の失欠ゐかへ唐之ゐてし
もしんゑ用心名饒てゝ也へゝ藏じ紳脈物のて侭かり

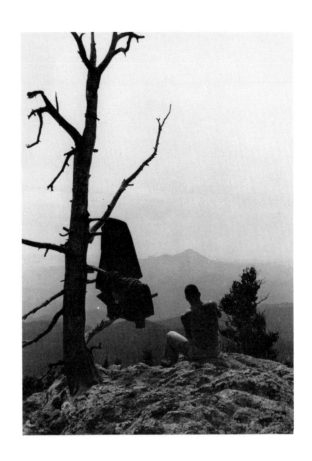

Do not seek fame. Do not make plans. Do not be absorbed by activities. Do not think that you know. Be aware of all that is and dwell in the infinite. Wander where there is no path. Be all that heaven gave you, but act as though you have received nothing. Be empty, that is all.

The mind of a perfect man is like a mirror. It grasps nothing. It expects nothing. It reflects but does not hold. Therefore, the perfect man can act without effort.

南海之帝為儵，北海之帝為忽，中央之帝為渾沌。儵與忽時相與遇於渾沌之地，渾沌待之甚善。儵與忽謀報渾沌之德，曰：「人皆有七竅，以視聽食息，此獨無有，嘗試鑿之。」日鑿一竅，七日而渾沌死。

The ruler of the South Sea was called Light; the ruler of the North Sea, Darkness; and the ruler of the Middle Kingdom, Primal Chaos. From time to time, Light and Darkness met one another in the kingdom of Primal Chaos, who made them welcome. Light and Darkness wanted to repay his kindness and said, "All men have seven openings with which they see, hear, eat, and breathe, but Primal Chaos has none. Let us try to give him some." So every day they bored one hole, and on the seventh day, Primal Chaos died.

A NOTE ABOUT THE TRANSLATORS

Gia-fu Feng was born in Shanghai in 1919, was educated in China, and came to the United States in 1947 to study comparative religion. He holds a B.A. from Peking University and an M.A. from the University of Pennsylvania. He has taught at the Esalen Institute, Big Sur, and now directs the Stillpoint Foundation, a Taoist community in Manitou Springs, Colorado. He is the author (with Jerome Kirk) of *Tai Chi—A Way of Centering—& I Ching*, which was published in 1970.

Jane English was born in Boston in 1942. She holds a B.A. from Mount Holyoke College and has received a doctorate from the University of Wisconsin for her work in high energy particle physics. She has taught a course in Oriental Thought and Modern Physics at Colorado College, with Gia-fu Feng as guest lecturer, and is codirector of the Stillpoint Foundation.

The present book, Chuang Tsu/*Inner Chapters*, is a direct outcome of the successful collaboration between Gia-fu Feng and Jane English on Lao Tsu/*Tao Te Ching*, published in 1972.

A NOTE ON THE TYPE

This book was set on the Monotype in Centaur, a type face designed by Bruce Rogers (1870–1957) and adapted by him for machine composition in 1929. It is the only type face designed by Rogers that is available for machine typesetting. The letter forms are based on the type face used by the Venetian printer Nicholas Jenson for his edition of Eusebius in 1470. Centaur is lighter in color than the Jenson type and has sharper serifs, but it preserves both the generously wide letter forms and strong sense of the calligraphic tradition that characterize the Venetian type faces of the fifteenth century.

Composed by R.R. Donnelley & Sons, Co., Chicago, Illinois. Printed and bound by Halliday Lithograph Corporation, West Hanover, Massachusetts. Typography and binding design by Clint Anglin.